# SCIENTIFIC OF HARRY LORD'S LIGHTNING JIU JITSU

By Marc Lawrence

# The 21 Universal Concepts of Human Hand to Hand & Hand-held Weapon Based Fighting

By Marc Lawrence

## Introduction

Every martial art was developed in time to answer a problem of fighting against an attacker. Each was developed in a time and place around specific clothing and equipment types, with specific social rules, terrain/surfaces and with or without weapons. Each developed solutions or answers to those kinds of attacks, each region came up with methods through observations and trial and error. As a student who studies their martial art as well as studying those other arts they have to fight, they will notice the common threads that make up all human fighting methods. This is the study of how humans fight is called Hoplology.

As you study each art I will describe in this series through my research a teacher's or founders material, you need to look for the universal common concepts and see what is missing in this art. This should lead you to the next question as to why was the method and system created? What were the social restrictions of the time and place? What were the terrain limitations? What clothing helped developed this art and what made this art ineffective? What were the weapons used or not used and if so why? The question should be would this martial art work well today or would need to be modified to today's time, social rules, terrains, and weapons?

As I have previously stated there are universal concepts of fighting, here are 21 Universal Concepts can be found used by all fighting arts throughout the world.

1. Know and understand your and your opponent's distance of reach at all times.
2. There are only five lines that make up the human body's geometry these are: right outside line right inside line center line, left inside line and left outside line.
3. There are only three main parts of the human body, these are the top- head to shoulder, middle from shoulders to hips, and bottom hips to legs. This is divided in half of from to back and down the center line in half. This makes areas to attack and defense.
4. There are only five ranges of fighting. These are: 1) out of range 2) long range 3) medium range 4) close range 5) wrestling/grappling range.
5. There are only four attacking pressures that can be applied when fighting as these are: Heavy Forward, Medium Forward Neutral and Reverse. Yes, these can be mixed but this is the basics.

6. There are only four basic body positions in fighting and there are: Standing, Crouching, Kneeling and On-the-ground, everything else is variation of these.
7. There are 11 basic weapons on the human body; these consist of 2 fists, 2 elbows, 2 knees, 2 feet, hips, head and teeth. All can be used in battle.
8. Fighting is like dance as it is about timing, rhythm and fluidity in motion. If any of these are not correct then the fighter will be defeated.
9. The human body can be disrupted from its upright position by four simple motions. These are: rotational, column disruption, base disruption and joint disruption.
10. The human body has a limited number of movements it can do this limiting what the attacks and defenses will be.
11. There are only so many effective targets on the human body; these are based upon the type of strike used or the type of weapon used.

12. There are four enemies in a fight that you must master: Surprise, Fear, Doubt and Confusion. Learn to use them against others.
13. There are only five basic types of strikes; forehand, backhand, thrust, upward and downward. Learn to use each of these effectively.
14. Strikes with weapons or limbs are simply linear, curving or thrusting learn to each correctly.
15. A fight can be rhythmic or broken rhythmic in its beat. This will help you when counter attacking.
16. Your attack will be direct or indirect in nature. Have plan understand the strengths and weakness of each.
17. There are eight basic human attack methods these are simply: projectile, stabbing/thrusting, slashing, impacting, strangle/choking, joint manipulation, pressure point-pain/nerve compliance. Know and understand all of these so that you have full tool box to draw from.

18. Guarding with weapons and hand to hand should be one of the following based upon your plan: Defensive, Offensive or Transitional.
19. There are only three basic guards with weapons and hand to hand, High Guard, Middle Guard and Low Guard based upon what part of the body is being attacked or is threatened. These guards are divided into Long range, Medium range, Close range and Wresting range. These are seen in Bare Knuckle Boxing, Classic Karate, Modern Boxing and BJJ.
20. There are only four methods of defense and these are simply: avoidance, deflection, parry/pass block/shielding. Know each of these and how to apply them at the right time.
21. Remember that blades, projectiles and impact weapons will beat your flesh and bones! Do not try and block sharp weapons, flying projectiles or heavy impact weapons! You will be damaged.

## *A FOREWORD BY THE AUTHOR*

YOU, *too, can be tough!* You can defeat your enemy in a fight. This is what LIGHTNING JU-JITSU promises you. Toughness and victory are what it can bring you.

In the pages of this book lie the secrets of Science over mere strength—technique over big but untaught muscles.

Man always has had to overcome obstacles huge in size. Our ancestors of prehistoric days lived in a world over-run by monsters who outweighed a man as you do a rabbit, and to whom Nature had given strength and weapons to crush a man as easily as you would a fly. Yet it is Man who is alive today while the monster kingdom perished thousands of years ago. Man could never have hoped to survive had he relied solely on his own puny strength to vanquish his terrifying enemies. Knowing this, he used his brain. He thought out means of overcoming the odds of weight and strength against him. He discovered that dumb beasts rush headlong and without reason and he learned to sidestep their mad lunge and send them through a flimsy camouflage of brush and over the side of a cliff to their doom. He learned to lure them to the edge of a pit where their weight and impetus would crash them to the bottom. He learned to hurl rocks that would crush their skulls and to fashion pointed shafts that would pierce their bodies. In a word, he called upon Science to reinforce his weak natural equipment, and he became the Giant among giants.

That is the essence of LIGHTNING JU-JITSU—to multiply your strength many times over by utilizing the ignorant strength and equipment of your foe. His weight, his size, the force of his rush and his weapons—these become yours, not his, in the fight. Even his clothing—the lapel of his coat, the heel of his shoe—are transformed into powerful allies for you and, if correctly employed, will guarantee your victory.

LIGHTNING JU-JITSU shows you how to accomplish this—simply, yet with deadly thoroughness. All you need do is apply yourself to learning its principles. Do this and mastery will soon be yours! Then you will enjoy the strength and confidence of knowing you are ready for any emergency—and tough enough to win.

H. L.

## *PREFACE*

OUT of the Orient—home of so many secrets—has come Ju-Jitsu, the secret art of hand-to-hand combat. Its origin is lost in time. Like so many other things the Japanese appropriated, it was probably imported from China, but altered and perfected over a period of centuries.

Until recently this secret deadly weapon was jealously guarded. Its knowledge was restricted to a single class of society—the *samurai*, aristocratic military caste of Japan. Commoners were prohibited from learning it. As a result, a young aristocrat could be an easy victor in any encounter with the "common herd." That was one way of asserting his superiority.

Even to the *samurai* the mysteries of Ju-Jitsu were not too freely revealed. Only after long training and apprenticeship were devotees initiated into the inner secrets—and then only on a sacred oath of silence.

Fortunately, Ju-Jitsu is no longer the exclusive weapon of the Japanese. It is available to everyone alert to its value in these hazardous times.

LIGHTNING JU-JITSU equips you with a potent defense and counter-attack against any intruder, bully, mugger, or gunman. It is equally effective for man or woman, civilian or soldier, policeman or guard. You don't need big muscles or superior weight to apply it. Technique does the trick.

A word of warning is necessary. Many of the methods revealed here are dangerous, even fatal. You are on your honor never to abuse your knowledge. Save it for the decisive moment when it counts. In a life-or-death contest, of course, no holds are barred.

You will find most of the defenses presume that your opponent will be right-handed. Of course, it is possible to execute any body movement on either side. Simply substitute left for right in the directions. In practising, learn to apply every defense both ways with equal facility, so that you will always be prepared.

The best way to practice is with a partner. To master any technique work first for precision, then speed. For the sake of clarity, the essential movements have been outlined as separate steps. Properly performed, these movements should become one rapid, continuous motion. Regular practice will make you an expert in LIGHTNING JU-JITSU.

## *CONTENTS*

*To*

*Science over brute strength*

# 1 *Principles of Lightning Ju-Jitsu*

## WHAT JU-JITSU MEANS

THE word *ju*, in the Japanese, means "gentle," "pliant," or "yielding," while *jitsu* is "art" or "practice." Put together, the term Ju-Jitsu can be translated as "the art of yielding or giving way."

Does this imply that Ju-Jitsu is a technique of non-resistance?

Far from it. Ju-Jitsu is a system not only of defense but of counter-attack. But instead of meeting an onslaught directly, force for force, you submit—or pretend to submit—in order to gain a calculated advantage over your opponent. You want to maneuver him into a position where his force and strength will work his own undoing. In other words, *you aim at a maximum result with a minimum effort.*

For example, should someone try pushing you as in Fig. 1, you withdraw, keeping your balance. Meanwhile your opponent, not meeting the expected resistance, is thrust off-balance by his forward lunge (Fig. 2), and thus presents an easy target for your counter-attack. A sudden tug of the sleeve and he is thrown to the ground (Fig. 3).

As for Ju-Jitsu being a "gentle art," you can mark that down to the diabolical Japanese humor.

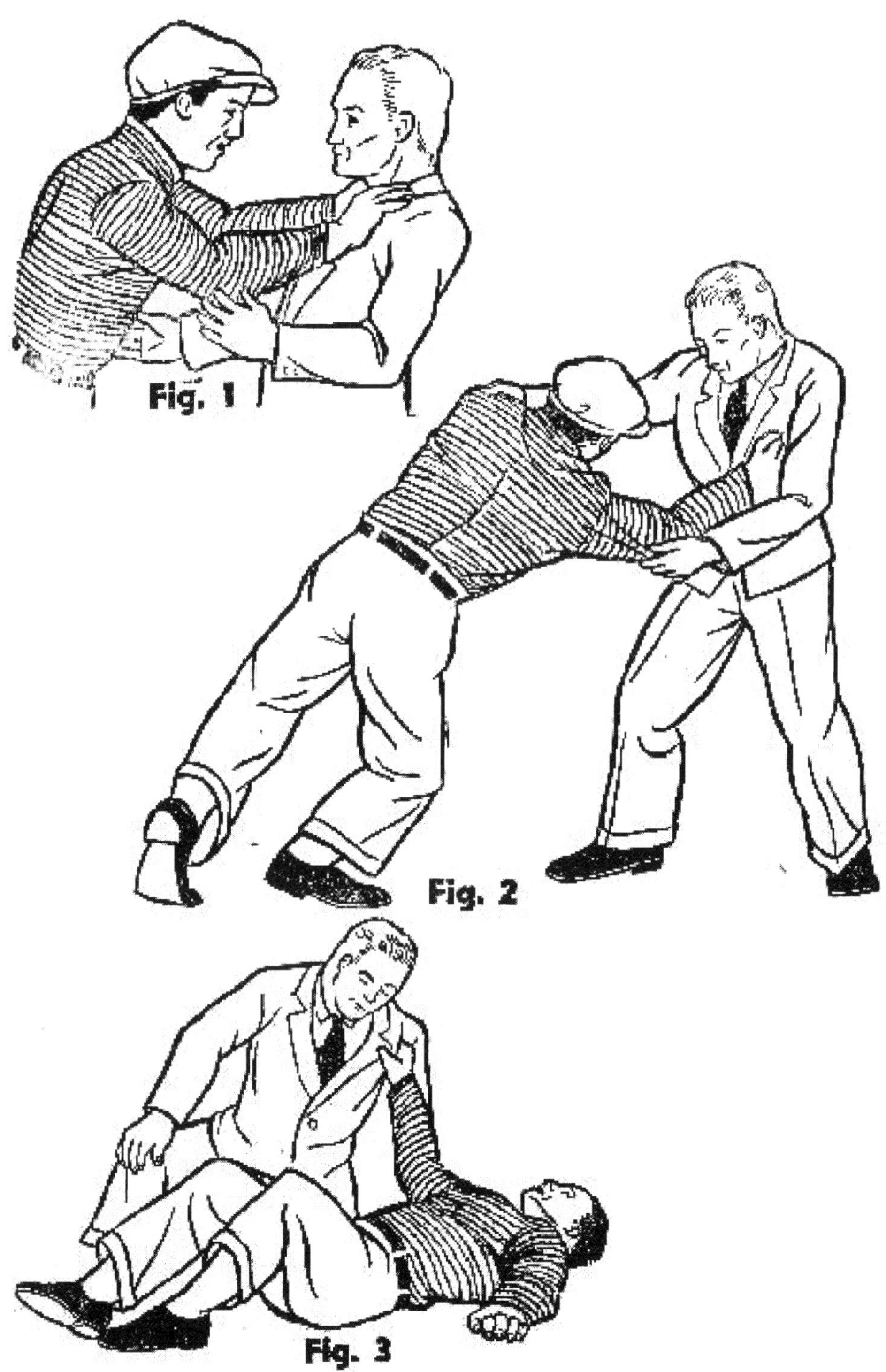

Fig. 1

Fig. 2

Fig. 3

## BALANCE

IT was "the last straw," you recall, "that broke the camel's back." Behind this saying is concealed a real physical truth. No matter how huge the weight, it can always be tipped by a finger—or a straw—at a certain point of balance.

The same principle applies to the human body. A man standing upright, with his feet planted firmly under him, is like a tree. He can not be moved except by an exertion of considerable force. But should his stance be unsteady, or should one of his feet be off the ground, it requires less effort to move him. *A person off-balance cannot defend himself properly. His weight and strength do not count.* That is why a child can sometimes tip a reeling drunkard.

Fig. 4 shows an ankle throw. The subject is being kicked as he is shifting his weight to the lifted foot before placing it on the ground. His balance is thereby broken and a slight pull at his clothing will throw him.

A substantial part of the technique of LIGHTNING JU-JITSU consists of shoving, pulling, twisting, or luring your opponent into an off-balance position in order to give him the "last straw" treatment.

Notice the word *luring*. This means feinting—concealing your intention—misdirecting your opponent to get him where you want him. You use your wits as much as your hands or feet.

The principle of balance is applied in almost every Ju-Jitsu move. Learn to recognize and use it.

Fig. 4

## LEVERAGE

WHETHER you realize it or not, you have been using lever most of your life. The scale, see-saw, windowpole, and crow bar are familiar examples. Briefly, a lever is a simple ma chine for transmitting and modifying force and motion The ancient Greek scientist, Archimides, is reputed to hav said, "Give me a lever and I'll move the world."

What has this got to do with Ju-Jitsu, you ask? Bein an instrument for motion, *the human body consists of a serie of lever—arms, legs, etc. You can use these levers to you advantage in hand-to-hand combat.*

Let's take a simple application. If you wanted to ge a good grip on your opponent's clothing in order to swin him around, you'd seize him at two widely-separated points such as the collar on one side and the sleeve on the other With this grip you could swing him more readily than i you held him by both lapels. The reason is wider leverage Common sense? Yes, but it's also science.

Look at Fig. 5. By thrusting his hip under his opponen the thrower makes it serve as an axis, or turning point- balancing half his opponent's body on each side. In othe words, you have here a lever of the see-saw type. Regardle of weight, a man in this position can be thrown with a twi of the hip or a tug of the sleeve. The see-saw lever (Fig. 6 is used in most throws.

The hold in Fig. 7 illustrates a different kind of leve Here the pressure applied at the wrist is being transmitte to the arm at a point just above the elbow. In the proce of transmission the pressure is multiplied, resulting in greater force than that originally exerted. The principle the same as using a crowbar when you cannot lift a sewer-t with your hands (Fig. 8). Remember—the longer the arm the lever, the greater the resulting force. You will find th principle operating in most pressure holds.

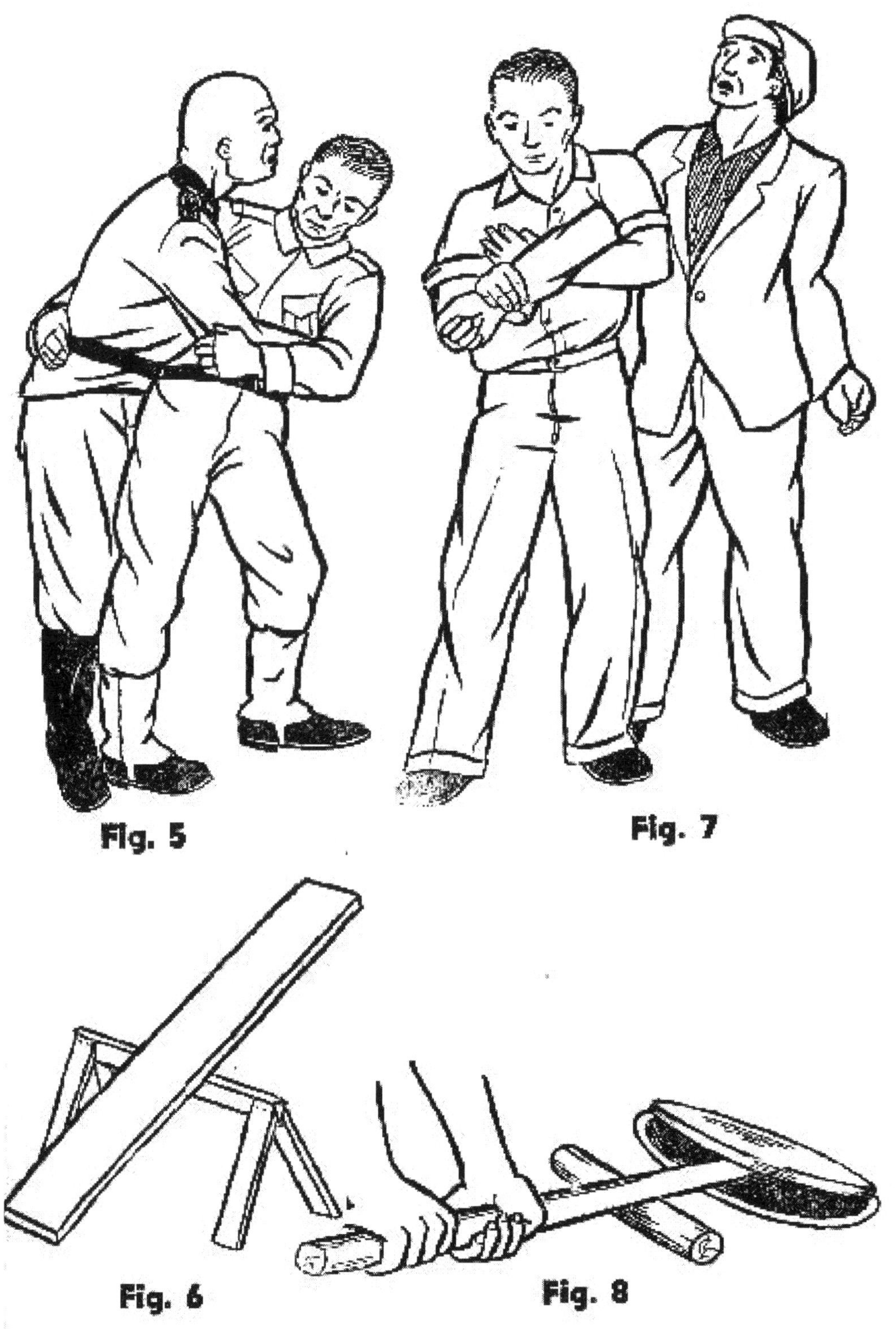

Fig. 5

Fig. 7

Fig. 6

Fig. 8

## HITTING WHERE IT HURTS

LIGHTNING JU-JITSU makes use of still another principle—striking your opponent where he is most vulnerable, hitting where it hurts. Some of the nerve centers of the body are near the surface and therefore easy to get at. In these spots even moderate pressure will cause considerable pain, *and a sharp jab, pinch, or blow that hits the mark will temporarily paralyze the whole surrounding area.*

The accompanying charts (Figs. 9 and 10) show some of the vital nerve centers of the body. Using the ball of your index finger, practice locating them on yourself, so that you can find them precisely and quickly. This knowledge will prove very useful in subduing an opponent.

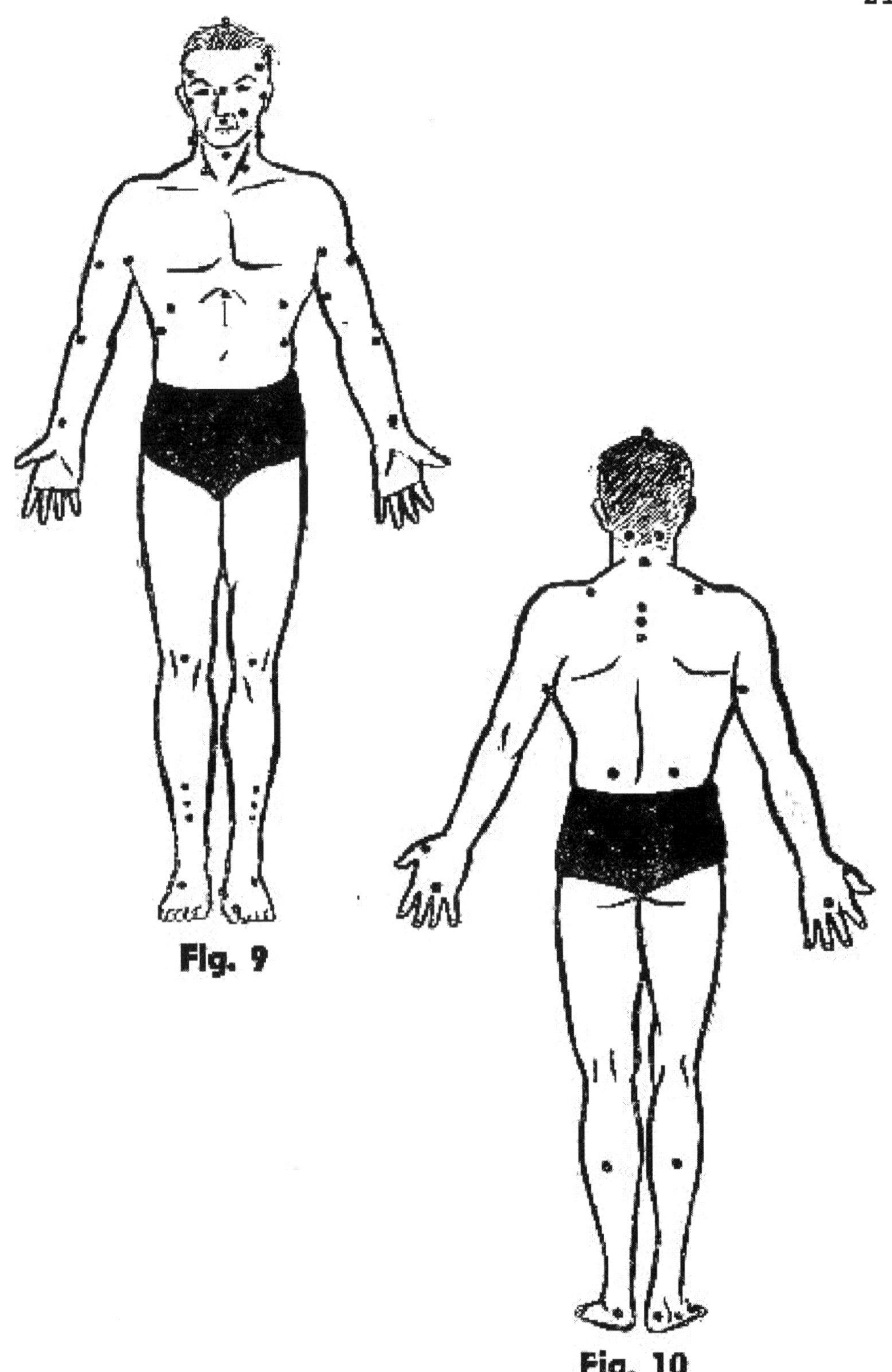

Fig. 9

Fig. 10

# 2 *Lightning Blows*

## EDGE-OF-THE-HAND BLOW

TO most people, the clenched fist has been the main weapon of attack or defense. But LIGHTNING JU-JITSU makes use of other blows more precise, painful, and deadly. The most frequent of these—the edge-of-the-hand blow—is delivered with the knife edge of the open hand; that is, the outer or little-finger side.

For a vertical blow, crook the arm at the elbow and swing it down obliquely with a swift, chopping motion. Keep the fingers rigid and close together (Fig. 11). Put your bodyweight behind the blow by rising to your toes; then flex your knees slightly at the instant of striking. Practice with either hand. Learn to strike so rapidly that your opponent cannot guess your intention.

For a horizontal blow, swing either hand out from the elbow in an arc. Keep the palm facing downward (Fig. 12).

Edge-of-the-hand blows are particularly effective in parrying an attacker's blow, in breaking his grip, in throwing him off-balance, and in inflicting punishment.

Apply these blows upon:

1. The wrist (especially when a fist or weapon is being aimed at you)
2. The lower or upper arm
3. The sides of the body

Except in a life-or-death struggle, avoid striking the following vital points where serious or even fatal injury may result:

1. The larynx or Adam's apple
2. The back of the neck
3. The sides of the neck
4. The kidneys or base of the spine

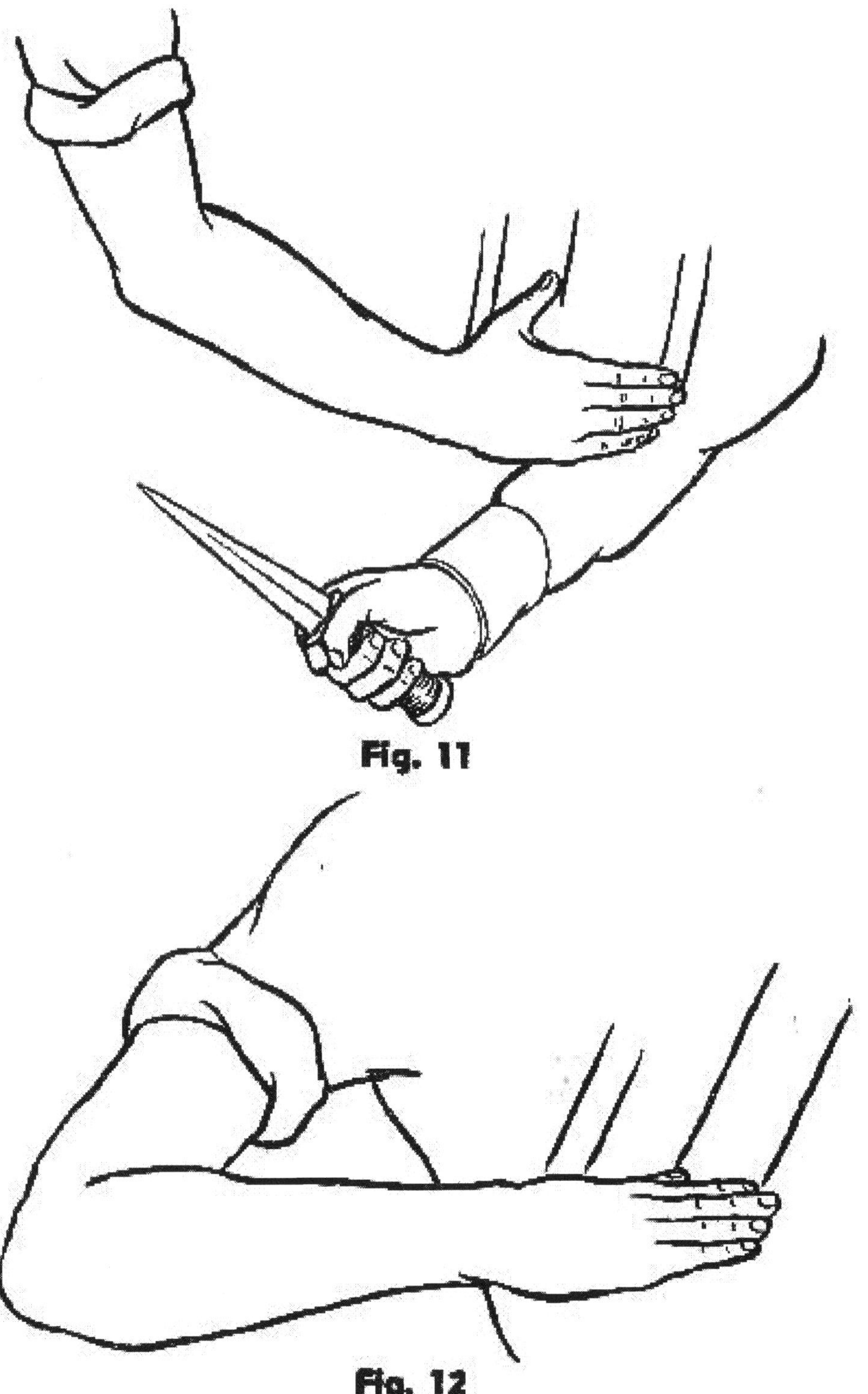

Fig. 11

Fig. 12

## TWO-FINGER JAB

WHEN directed at the right spot, a simple jab of the fingers produces a sharper, more concentrated pain than a fist blow which spreads the shock over too wide an area.

Use the index and middle fingers, keeping the other fingers locked back behind the thumb (Fig. 13). Move your hand from the bent elbow. At the moment of striking, twist your wrist so that the fingers bore in, like a bit eating into a board.

This jab should be applied against a soft spot covering vital nerves. A sensitive place is the delicate network of nerves over the stomach known as the *solar plexus*, a term made famous by Ruby Bob Fitzsimmons. Another vulnerable area is the flesh under the outer sides of the jawbone. See Fig. 9 and Fig. 10 for other nerve centers.

## KNUCKLE JAB

A further method of jabbing is with the middle knuckle of the second finger. Clench your fist, then extend your second finger a little so that the middle knuckle juts out (Fig. 14). When striking, twist the wrist in order to dig the knuckle in. While not quite as sharp as the finger, the knuckle will not bend against pressure.

Use this jab against nerve centers. A knuckle ground into your opponent's kidney will produce agonizing pain, and can fell him to the ground. Learn to locate the exact spot but be careful when practising.

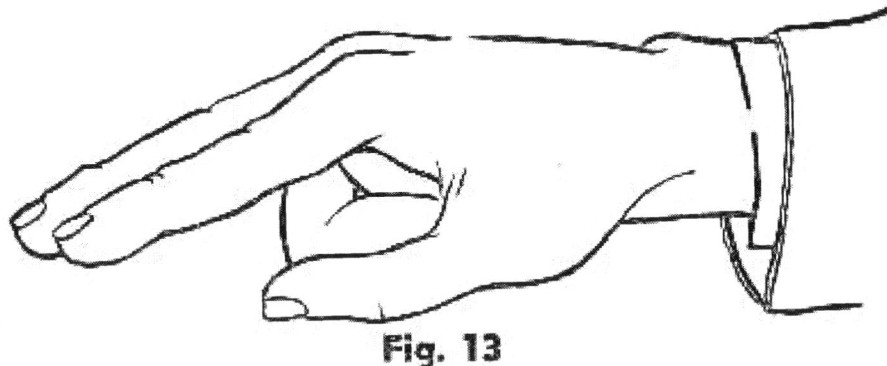

Fig. 13

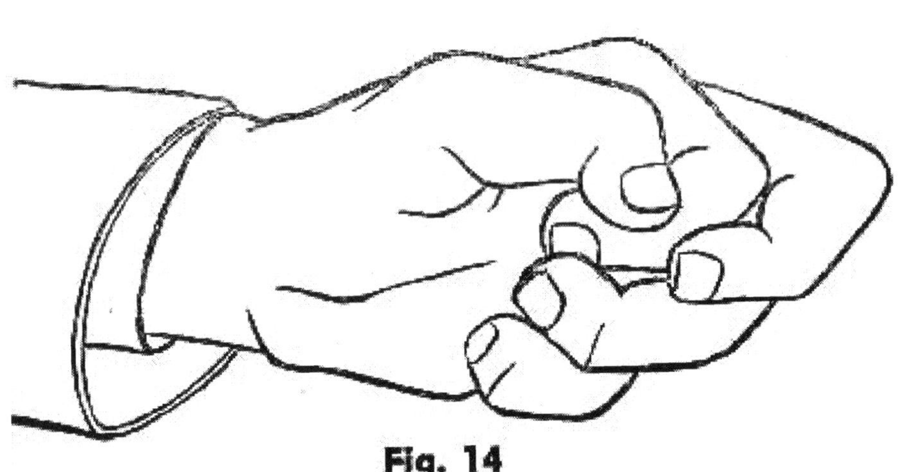

Fig. 14

## SHOULDER PINCH

You can paralyze your opponent's arms with the shoulder pinch. To apply from the front:

1. Bore your thumb into the hollow under the collar bone where it meets the socket of the upper arm.
2. Press your fingers into the back of his shoulder so as to cause a pinch (Fig. 15).

To apply the pinch from behind:

1. Set your fingers under the collar bone.
2. Press your thumb into the nerve center on the back of the shoulder, slightly below the base of the neck (Fig. 16).

If your opponent should attempt to kick you from this position, jab your knee into his back.

Fig. 15

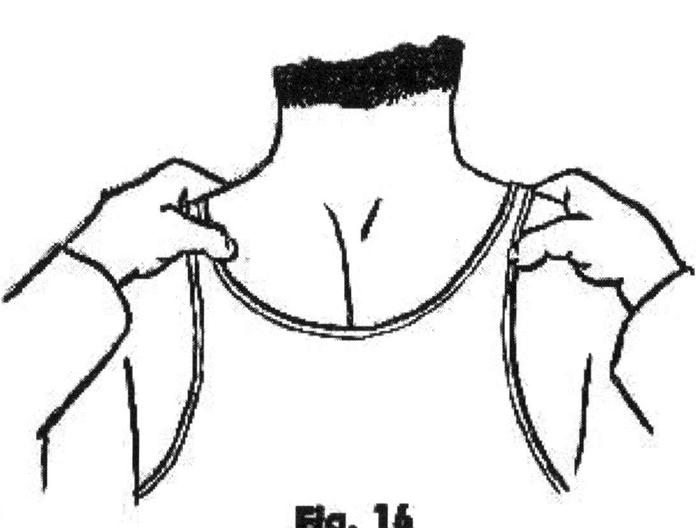

Fig. 16

## TEETH-RATTLER

EVEN the heel of the hand (Fig. 17) becomes a potent weapon when directed against your opponent's chin.

1. Keep your elbow bent, hand open, fingers spread, knees slightly flexed to put the weight of your body behind the blow.
2. With a sudden upward thrust, catch your opponent's chin in the heel of your hand, straighten your knees, and shove back vigorously (Fig. 17A).

You can apply this blow only at close quarters. If your opponent is too tall for you, bring him down with a knee jab to his groin.

## BOXING THE EARS

With your fingers close together and your hands cupped like a shell, you can strike your opponent's ears such a blow as to daze—and possibly deafen—him.

1. If possible, get behind your opponent to surprise him so that you won't be kicked.
2. Simultaneously, box both his ears with your cupped hands (Fig. 18).

Even a few pounds of force may shatter an eardrum. Try this blow very lightly on yourself to judge its effect. Do not use this method in an ordinary encounter. Reserve it for extremities.

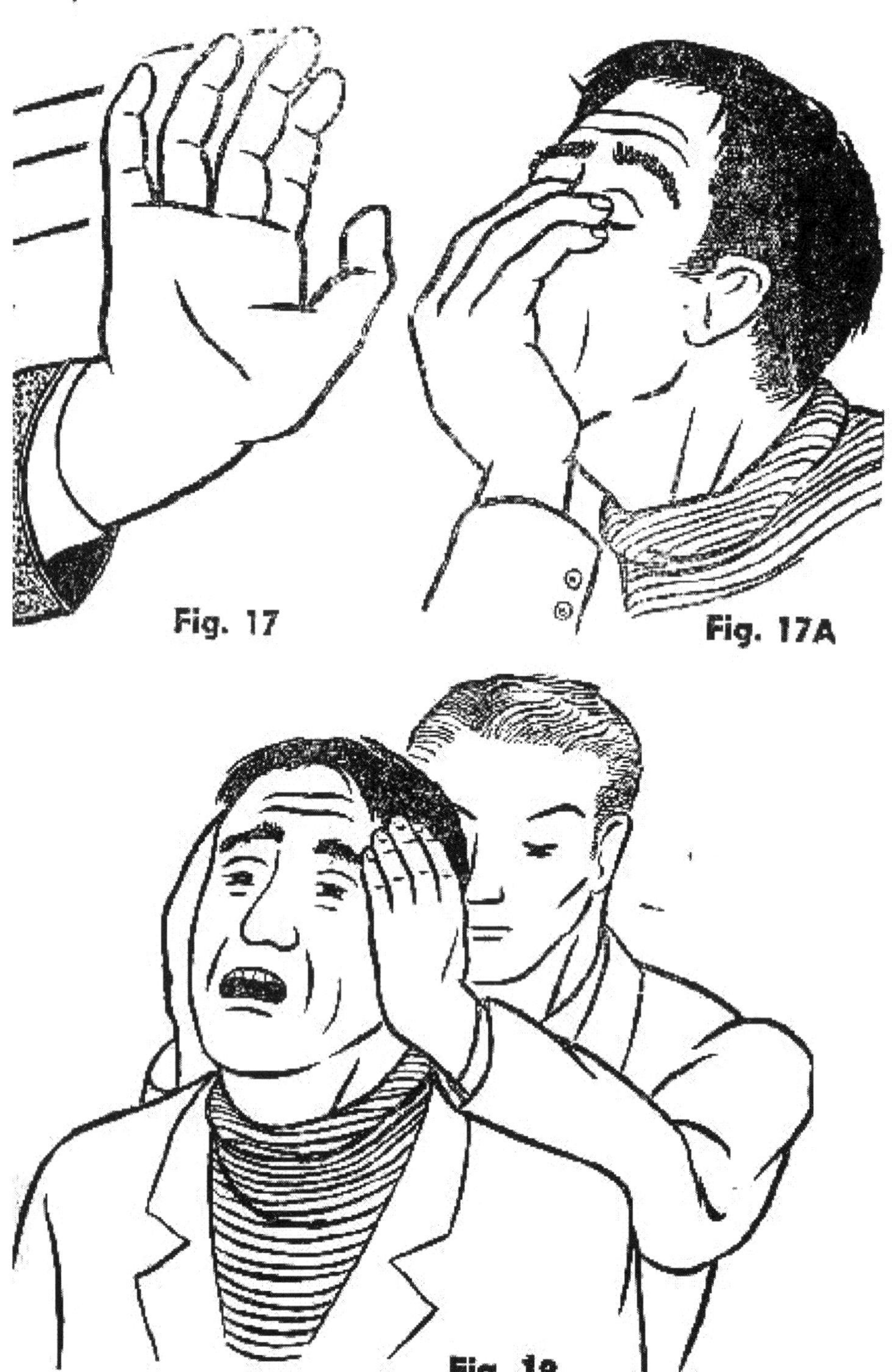

Fig. 17

Fig. 17A

Fig. 18

## ELBOW JAB

THE sharp bone protruding at the end of the elbow can deliver a wicked jab. When fighting at close quarters, watch for a chance to apply it against the sides of your opponent's body. Proper use of the elbow can also help you break through a crowd quickly.

1. Start with the elbow close to the body and your hand on the opposite shoulder. This position will give you space to swing.
2. Swiftly thrust your elbow out to the side in an arc Fig. 19).

## KNEE JAB

When closely pressed in a fight, it is almost instinctive to drive the knee upward into your opponent's groin or stomach. To deliver this blow forcefully:

1. Keep your weight on one leg.
2. Rock back on the heel of the other foot, dipping the knee a little.
3. Shoot the knee straight up (Fig. 20).

The blow is so painful as to cause a man to crumple up; it may injure him permanently.

To guard against such a blow from an opponent, learn to fight somewhat to his side, so that you are in a position to knee him, if necessary, but making it impossible for him to retaliate.

Fig. 19

Fig. 20

# 3 Grips, Twists, and Hold

## COAT GRIP

BOXERS and wrestlers ignore clothing. This is a big mistak because it limits the techniques of combat.

Ju-Jitsu—always the science—is more realistic. The pres ence of clothing makes possible a variety of movement which could not otherwise be executed. You will find, there fore, that you are often asked to get a grip on your opponent's clothing before "going to work" on him.

To do this properly:

1. Keep the palm of your hand toward you, thumb on top, fingers extended sidewards.
2. Catch a sizeable hunk of your opponent's garment between fingers and thumb (Fig. 21). Do not try to grasp his skin, too, as this will weaken your grip.

When applied to a substantial garment, such as a man's coat or jacket, this hold is almost impossible to shake. Obviously, it cannot be used on something flimsy which would tear in the fight.

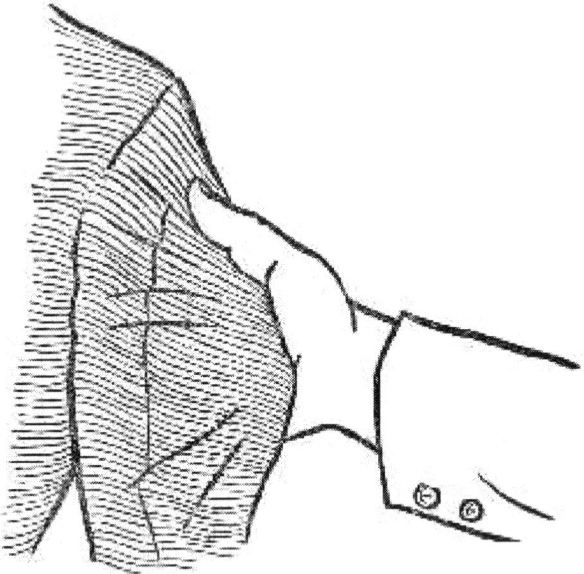

Fig. 21

## BOUNCER GRIP

TO evict an unwelcome visitor from an office or store, avoiding fuss, the following method is recommended:

1. Get behind the intruder.
2. With one hand, grab his collar; with the other, the seat of his trousers. He will be lifted onto his toes (Fig. 22). Any resistance would land him flat on his face.

Fig. 22

## THUMBSCREW (With One Hand)

THE thumbscrew, you recall, is an old instrument of torture based on the knowledge that the thumb is easily vulnerable. Ju-Jitsu also makes use of this fact with a simple, effective method for escorting an unwilling subject—or prisoner—wherever you want to take him.

1. Place your palm flush against his and fold your fingers (except the thumb) around the back of his hand.
2. Wrap your thumb around his and dig into the wedge between his thumb and index finger.
3. Press your fingers firmly into the back of his hand below the thumb and twist his thumb back with yours (Fig. 23).

## THUMBSCREW (With Both Hands)

1. Lock your fist around opponent's thumb (Fig. 24).
2. Simultaneously, seize his fingers with your other hand. Bend his fingers down and his thumb backwards. This will put him at your mercy (Fig. 25). If you wish, you can throw him by shoving him back unexpectedly.

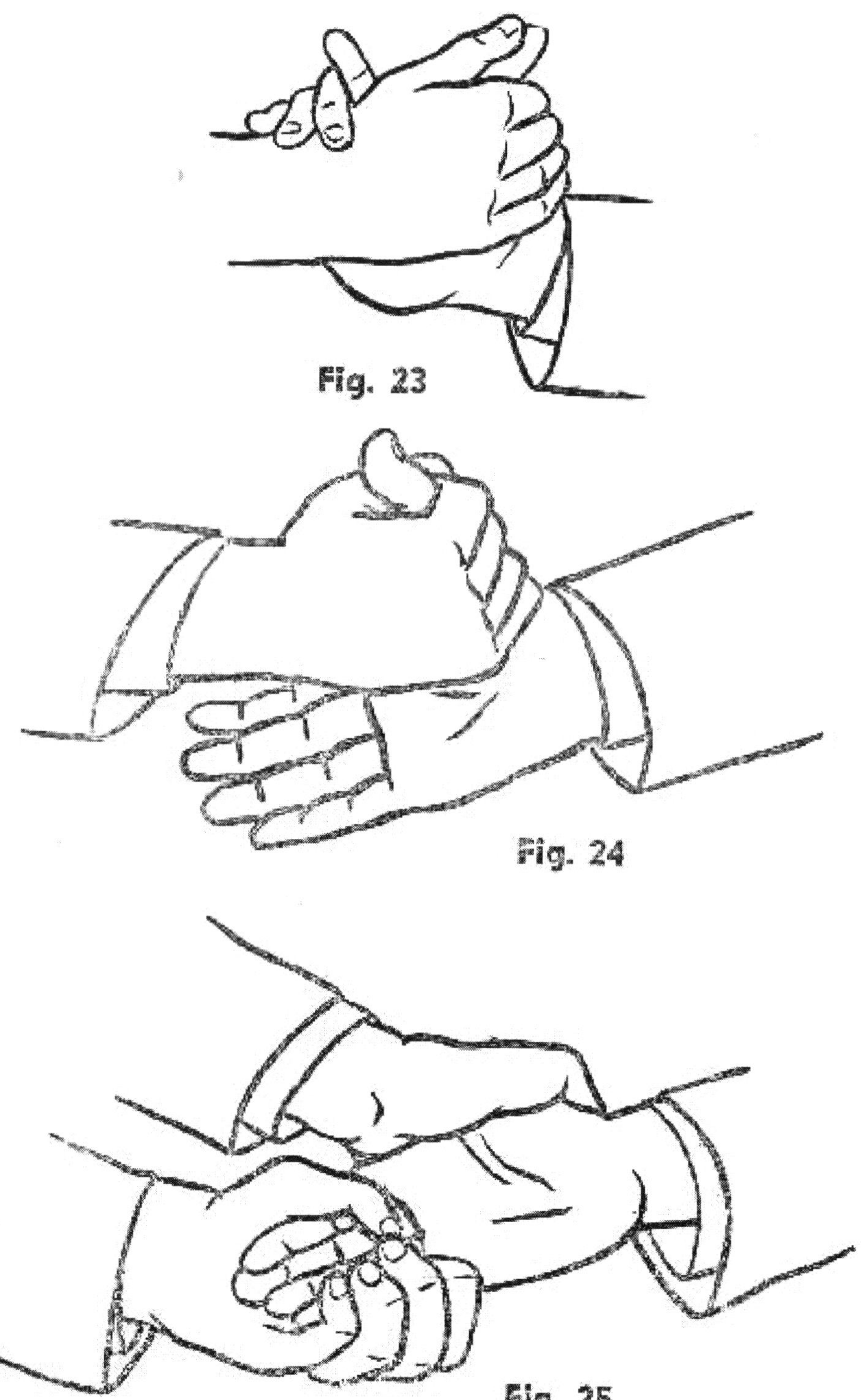

Fig. 23

Fig. 24

Fig. 25

## STRANGLE HOLD

1. You are facing your opponent. Capture his right wrist in your own right hand, using an underhand grip (thumb on top, as in Fig. 26).
2. Pivoting on your right foot, swing back so that you are directly behind him, twisting the wrist as you turn.
3. Thrust your left arm around his neck, strangling him between your armpit and elbow (Fig. 27).

## STRANGLE HOLD (Applied from the Rear)

1. Stand behind and a little to the left of your opponent.
2. Fling out your right arm to catch his chin, forcing it down and in against his throat.
3. Simultaneously, with your other hand grip his left wrist so that you can brace your chest against his body (Fig. 28).

Both these methods may kill a man in short order. In practising, learn the positions, but be extremely careful not to use pressure.

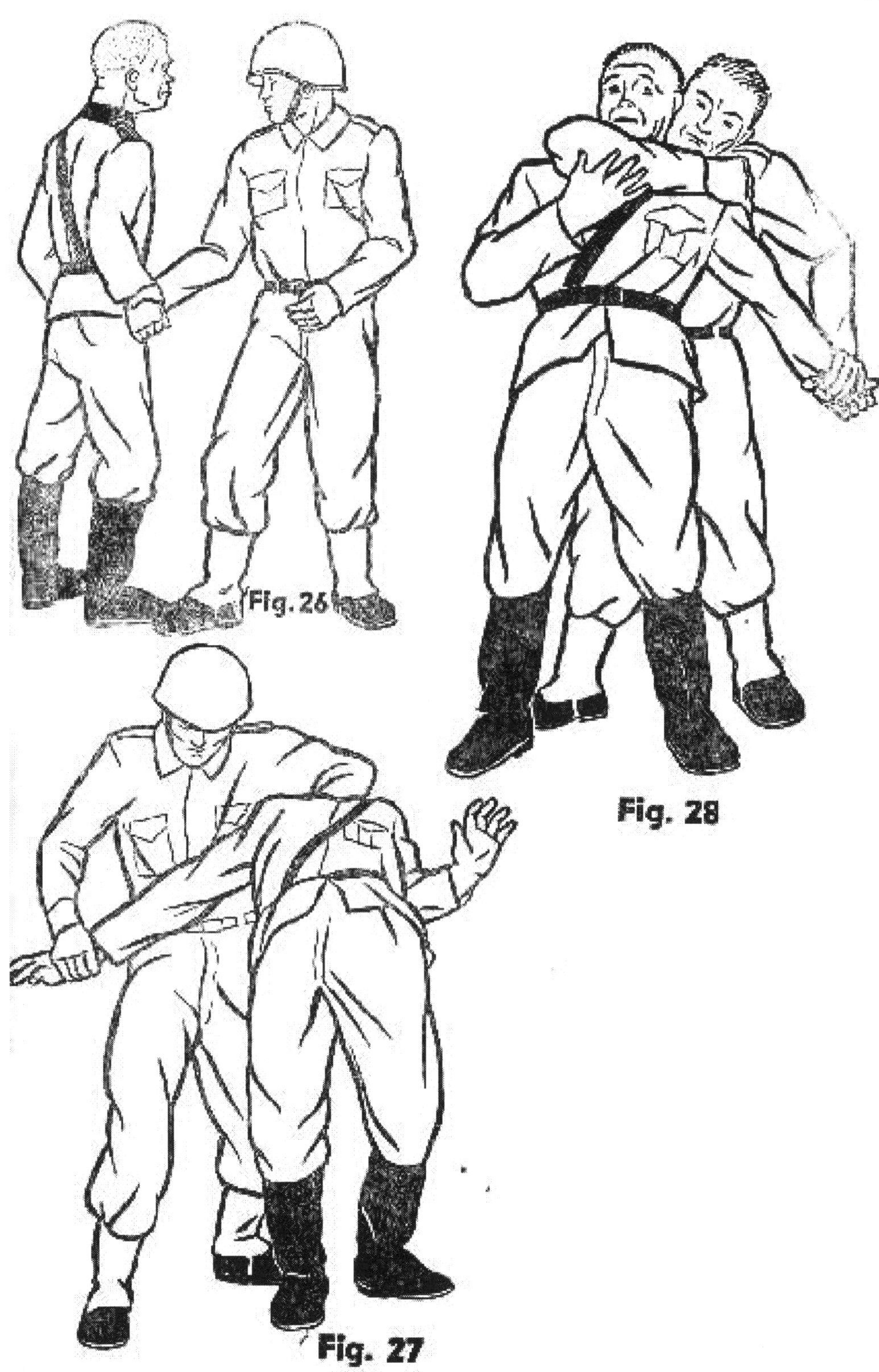

Fig. 26

Fig. 28

Fig. 27

# 4 *Throwing Your Foe*

## SCIENCE—NOT SIZE

ALTHOUGH it is easily possible to subdue an adversary without throwing him, there is nothing that takes the fight out of a man quicker—nothing so conclusively humiliating—as an unexpected fall. Also, while on the ground, he cannot defend himself effectively; you can pin him down any way you choose.

Ju-Jitsu throws do not require weight or strength but rather agility. You can throw any opponent by making him use his own weight to throw himself. You push, pull, or strike him in such a way as to knock him off-balance; and then you kick his feet from under. Or you maneuver into a position where you can balance his body like a see-saw; then let a sudden tug and the force of gravity do the rest.

In practising these throws remember that, although the steps are outlined separately, you must learn to make your action continuous. It should take only a few seconds to throw someone.

Remember also to practice on an exercise mat, a thick carpet, or a plot of grass.

When throwing a man, you can usually let him down easy or hard, as you choose. If you throw him violently onto a city pavement, you may crack his skull. Go easy—unless you've been given sufficient reason!

Fig. 29

## HIP THROW

YOUR opponent leans forward to attack you.

1. Slide your left foot inside his, so that his toes and yours are parallel. Keep your leg stiff and close up to him (Fig. 30).
2. Turn swiftly right. Use your left hand to squeeze his waist on the right side. Clutch his upper arm with your right hand and jerk your hips suddenly to the right (Fig. 31).
3. At the same time, tug firmly with your right hand and you will toss him over and down (Fig. 32).

Fig. 30

Fig. 32

Fig. 31

## SHOULDER THROW (A)

YOUR opponent approaches with right fist upraised.

1. Ward off the blow by grasping his wrist with your left hand. Move your right foot in close to his (Fig. 33).
2. Raise his arm while pivoting left on your right foot. This will bring your shoulder under his arm (Fig. 34).
3. Grab his right shoulder and pull down with both hands. As you bend forward, he will come somersaulting over your shoulder (Fig. 35).

If you move fast, this is a swell defense against a right hook.

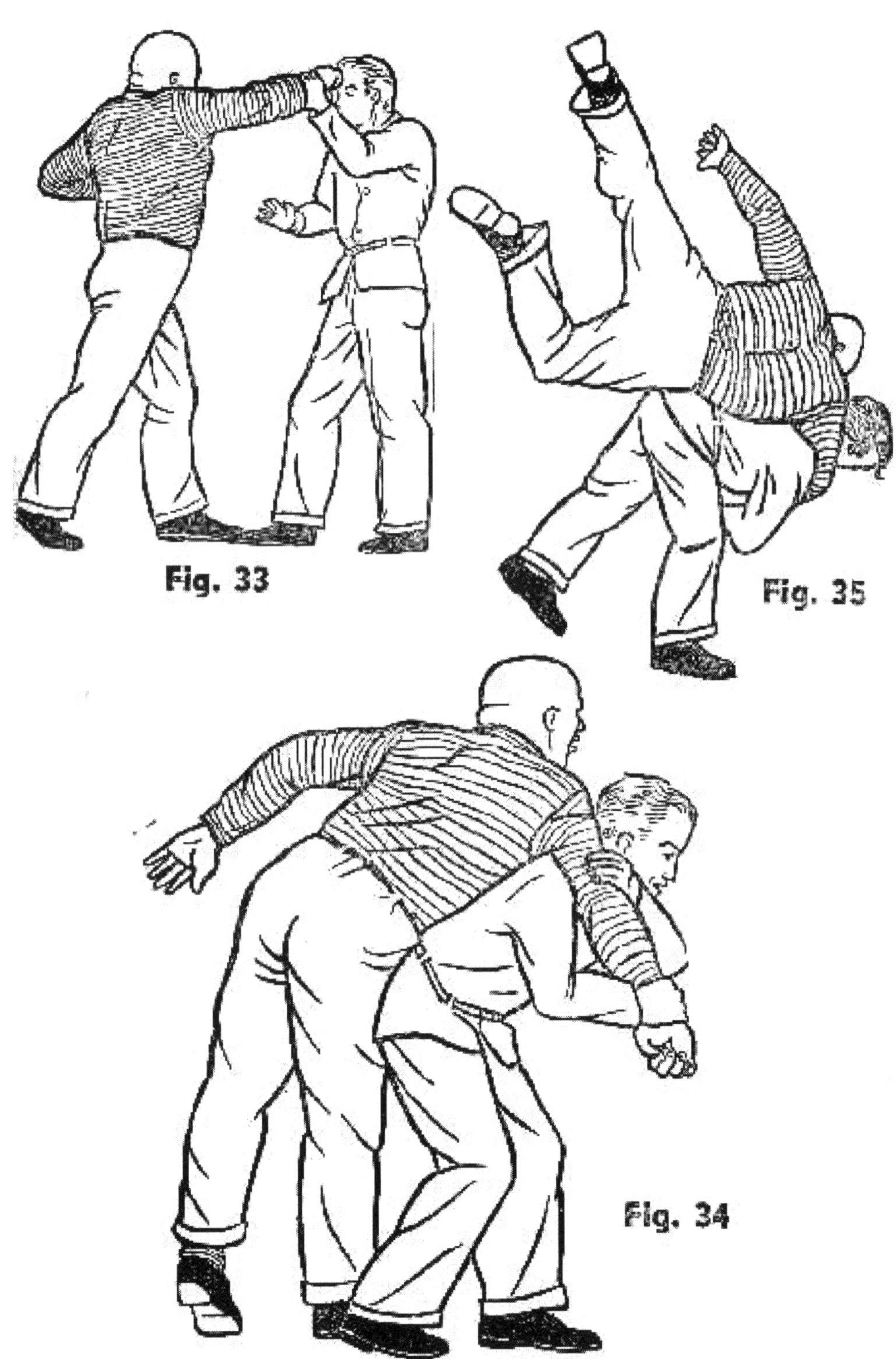
Fig. 33
Fig. 35
Fig. 34

## SHOULDER THROW (B)

YOUR opponent has a club in his right hand—and he has raised it menacingly.

1. Quickly close your left hand around his upraised wrist, keeping the thumb underneath. Simultaneously, grab him under the arm with your other hand (Fig. 36).

2. Swing around on your left foot and hoist his arm over your shoulder. Then bend quickly from the hip, forcing his arm down as far as it will go (Fig. 37). This action will pitch him over your head.

3. Pin him down securely by stepping on his neck. If you twist his wrist inward, he will have to drop the club (Fig. 38).

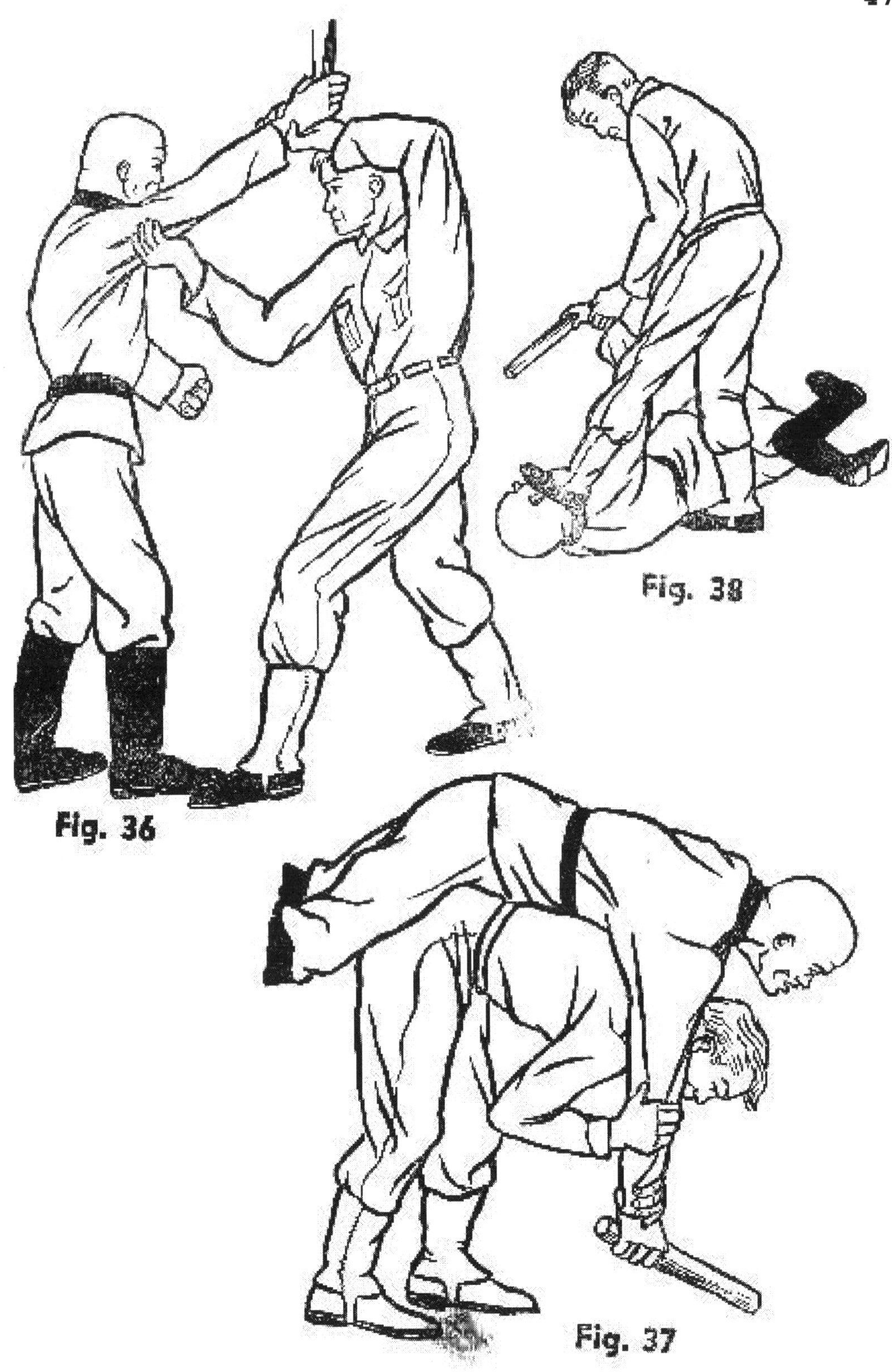
Fig. 36
Fig. 37
Fig. 38

## CHIN THROW

YOU are facing your opponent.

1. Bring the heel of your right hand swiftly up. (Fig. 39).
2. Catch your opponent's chin on the left side of his face and jam your left foot over his right while you continue shoving his face toward the right (Fig. 40).
3. As soon as he is well off-balance, kick his remaining prop from under him with your left foot. This movement will throw him (Fig. 41).

Fig. 40

Fig. 41

Fig. 39

## KNEE THROW

YOUR opponent is reaching into his right pocket for a knife or gun.

1. Step in on your left foot and grab his wrist with your left hand (Fig. 42).
2. Yank his arm forward. At the same time, seize his captured hand with your right hand, placing your fingers across the palm and your thumb underneath (Fig. 43).
3. With your left foot administer a sharp kick to the back of his right knee, and simultaneously transfer your wrist grip to his right hand (Fig. 44).
4. Tug firmly with both your hands and he will topple over backwards (Fig. 44A).

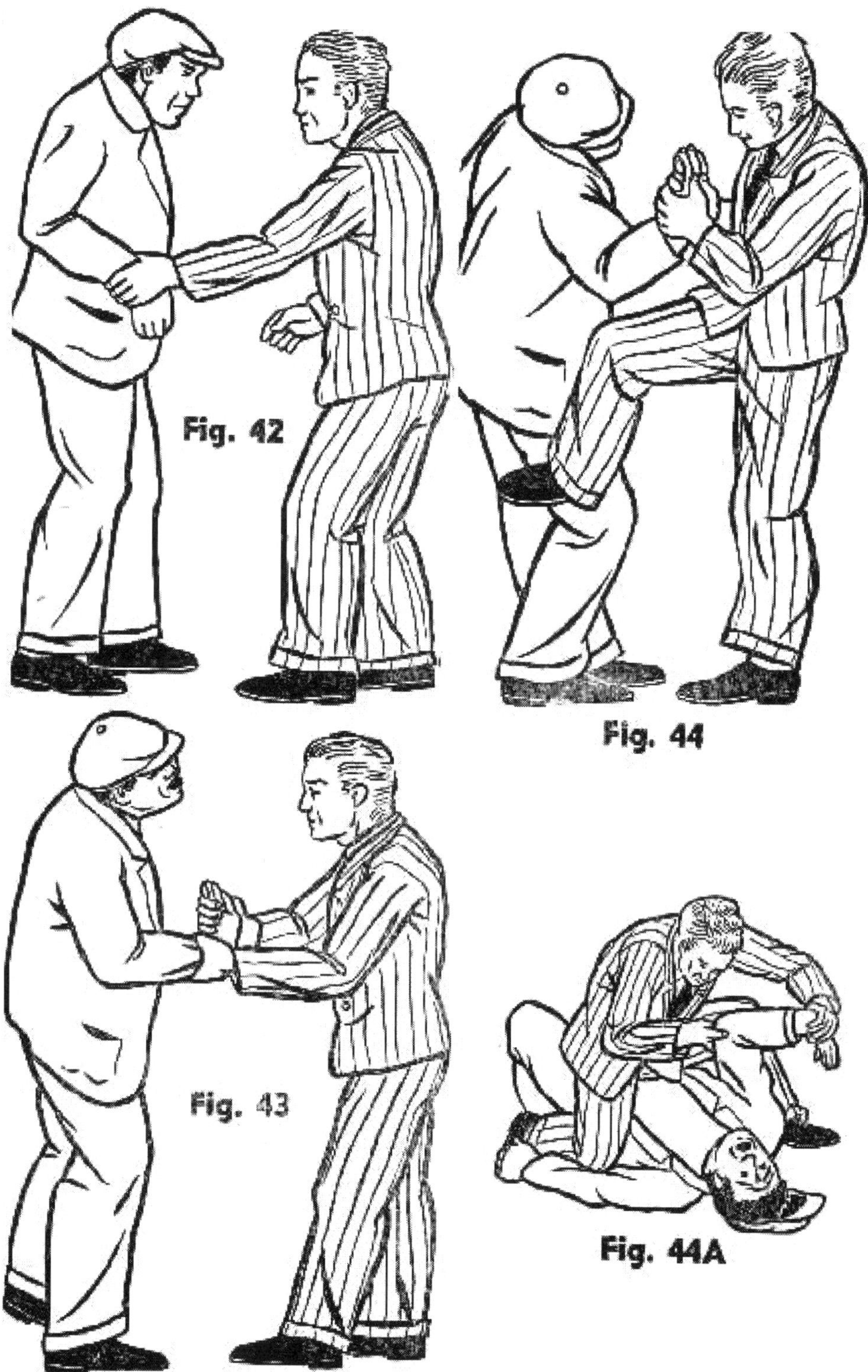

Fig. 42

Fig. 43

Fig. 44

Fig. 44A

## ANKLE THROW

YOU are facing your opponent.

1. Grasp his left lapel with your right hand and with your left hand clutch the back of his right sleeve at the upper arm. This position will give you wide leverage for your next move (Fig. 45).
2. Starting with your right foot, take three backward steps. As you take the first step, tug slightly with your right hand so that your opponent will make his first step forward with his left foot. On your second step, tug with the left hand, etc.
3. As your opponent lifts his right foot to make his fourth forward step, do not step backward as before. Swinging your left foot from the hip, use the sole of your shoe to kick his upraised ankle. At the same moment, pull to your left and downward with both hands (Fig. 46). He will fall to the ground.

The whole secret of tripping lies in the timing. In this case, you've got to kick your opponent's ankle while it is off the floor; that is, while his weight is being shifted, and at the same time pull him down on the same side. The backward steps described above are not necessary except to get him to raise the desired foot and to catch him at the precise moment of weight-shifting. However, if you are alert, you will find many opportunities to use this trip in any rough-and-tumble fight, even without going through the preliminaries. Just remember to use your left foot against his right, and vice versa.

Fig. 45

Fig. 46

# 5 *Breaks and Counters*

## BREAKING A WRISTLOCK (One Hand Caught)

YOUR opponent has seized one of your wrists with both his hands.

1. Use your free hand to inflict an edge-of-the-hand blow on his top wrist (Fig. 47).
2. Follow up with another blow on his under wrist.

## BREAKING A WRISTLOCK (Both Hands Caught)

TO make it easier to follow, this release is described and illustrated for one hand only, but the same procedure is to be used if both your wrists are caught.

1. Your opponent has gripped your wrist, as in Fig. 48.
2. Quickly twist your wrist inward as far as possible, turning it against his thumb (Fig. 49).

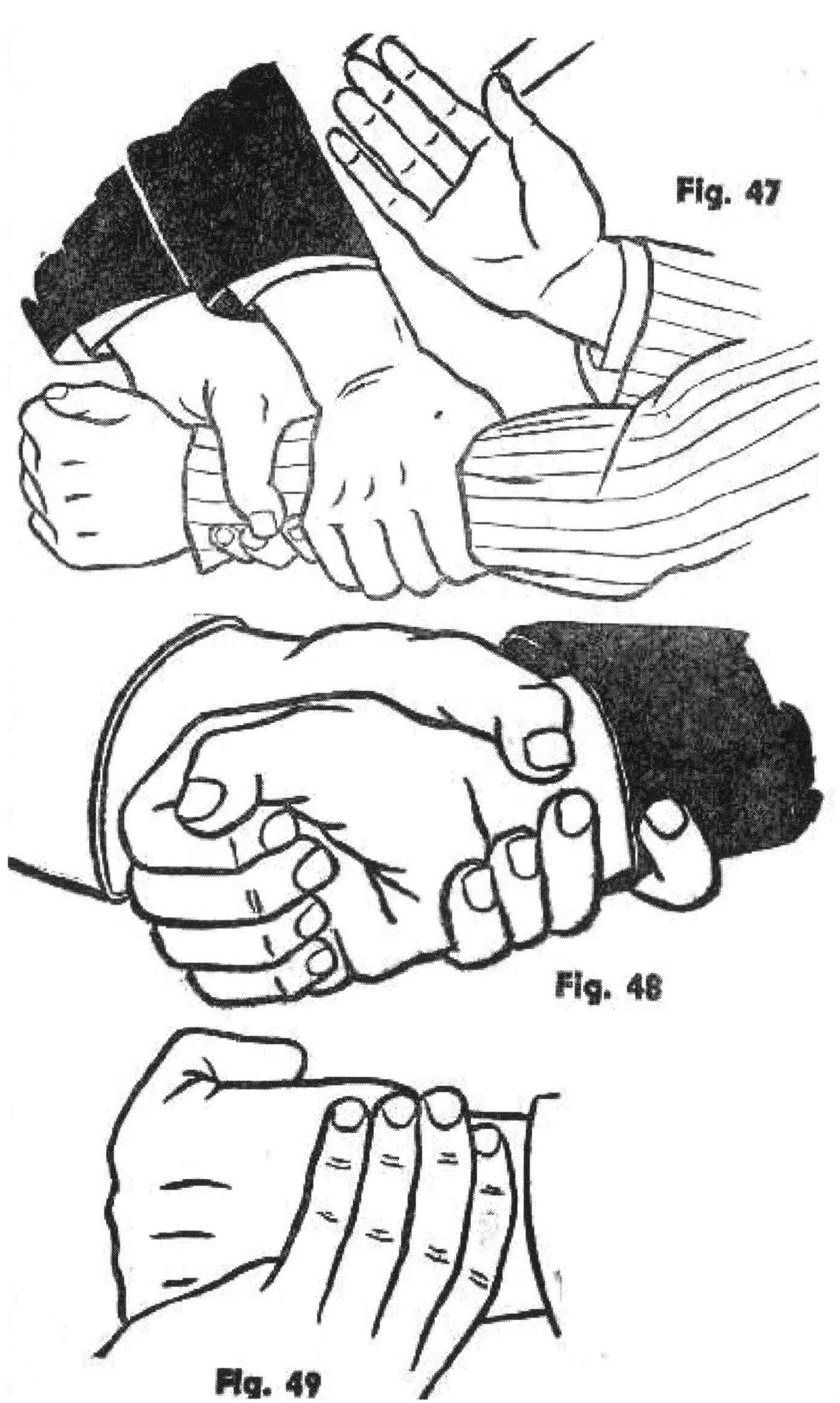

Fig. 47

Fig. 48

Fig. 49

## BREAKING A BODY GRIP (Front)

YOUR opponent has gripped you around the waist, imprisoning your arms.

1. Apply the knuckle jab to his solar plexus or groin with your right hand; with your other hand, jab his right shoulder blade (Fig. 50).
2. Thrust your right foot behind his left so that your heel is flush against his. Pushing suddenly, drive his foot forward and upward. He will topple over backwards (Fig. 51).

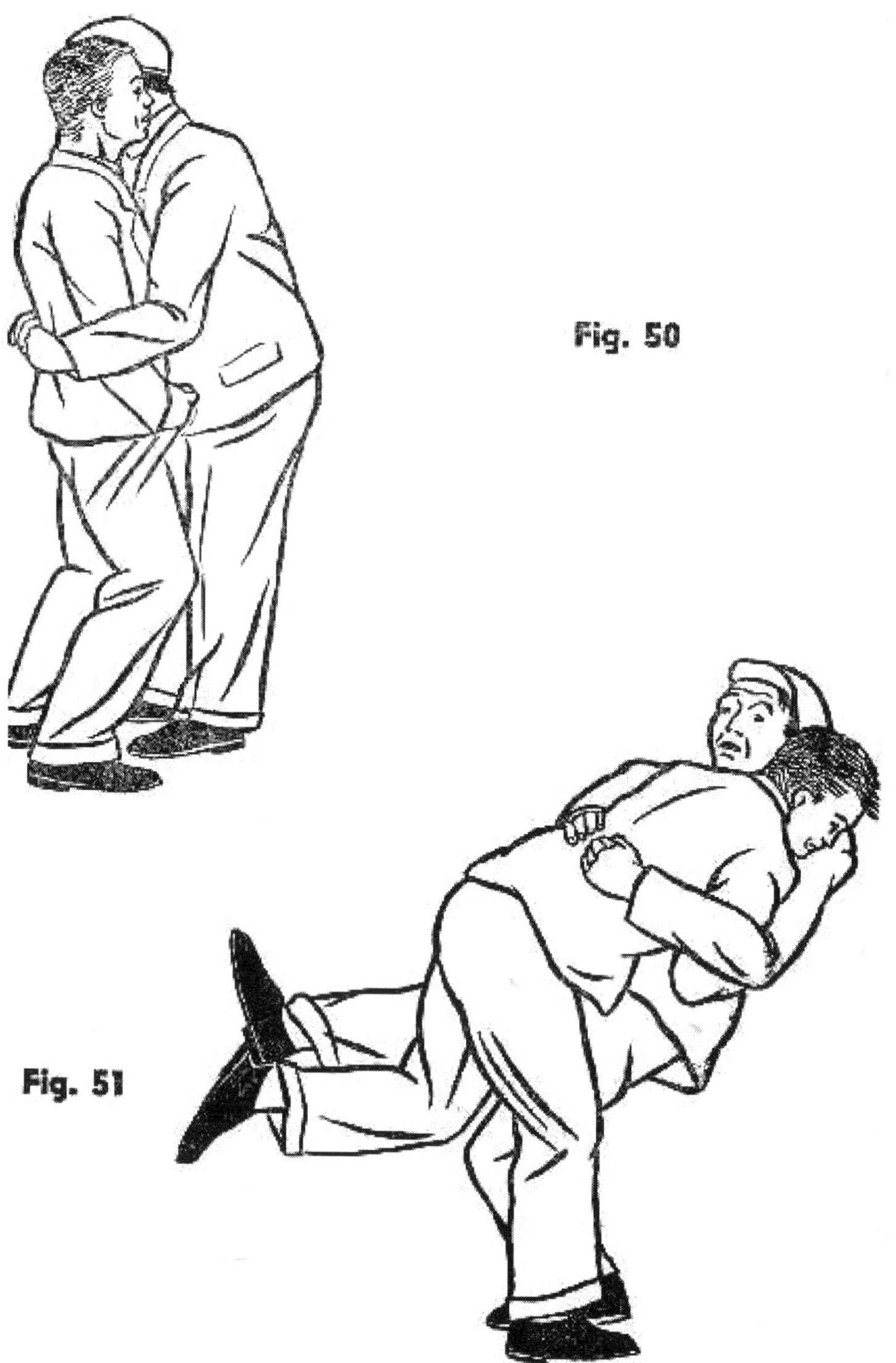

Fig. 50

Fig. 51

## BREAKING A BODY GRIP (Rear)

YOUR opponent has come up from the rear, gripping you around the waist. Your arms are free.

1. Move back slightly with one foot and bend forward from the waist (Fig. 52).
2. Grab one of your opponent's ankles (Fig. 53).
3. Pull it up as you suddenly sit down on top of him. Holding his heel in one hand, twist his toes with the other (Fig. 54).

Fig. 53

Fig. 52

Fig. 54

## BREAKING A STRANGLE HOLD (Front)

YOUR throat is clutched as in Fig. 55.

1. Clasp your hands and suddenly shoot them up and out, breaking the hold (Fig. 56).
2. Lock your fingers behind your opponent's neck, pulling his head forward and downward (Fig. 57).
3. Step back, hauling him with you. A sudden yank will send him to the floor (Fig. 58).

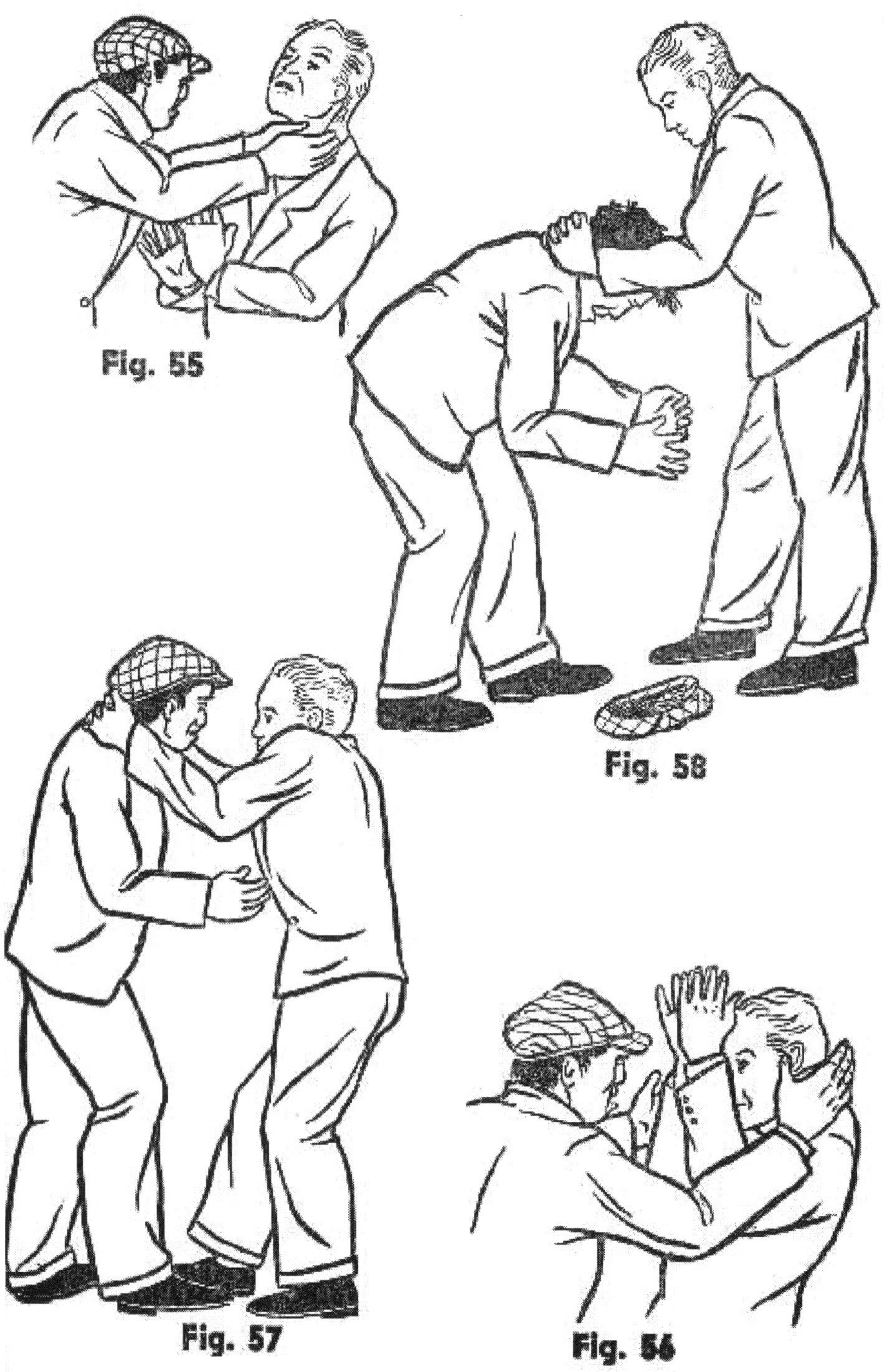

Fig. 55

Fig. 58

Fig. 57

Fig. 56

## BREAKING A STRANGLE HOLD (Rear)

YOU are being choked, as in Fig. 59.

1. Immediately tighten your neck muscles. This will give you precious seconds in which to act. It doesn't take long to be strangled.
2. Grip your opponent's wrists and twist them outward. His hold will be broken (Fig. 60).
3. Swiftly hoist his arms over your shoulders and dip forward from the hips (Fig. 61). With a good grip on his wrists you can fracture his arms when you pitch him forward on his head.

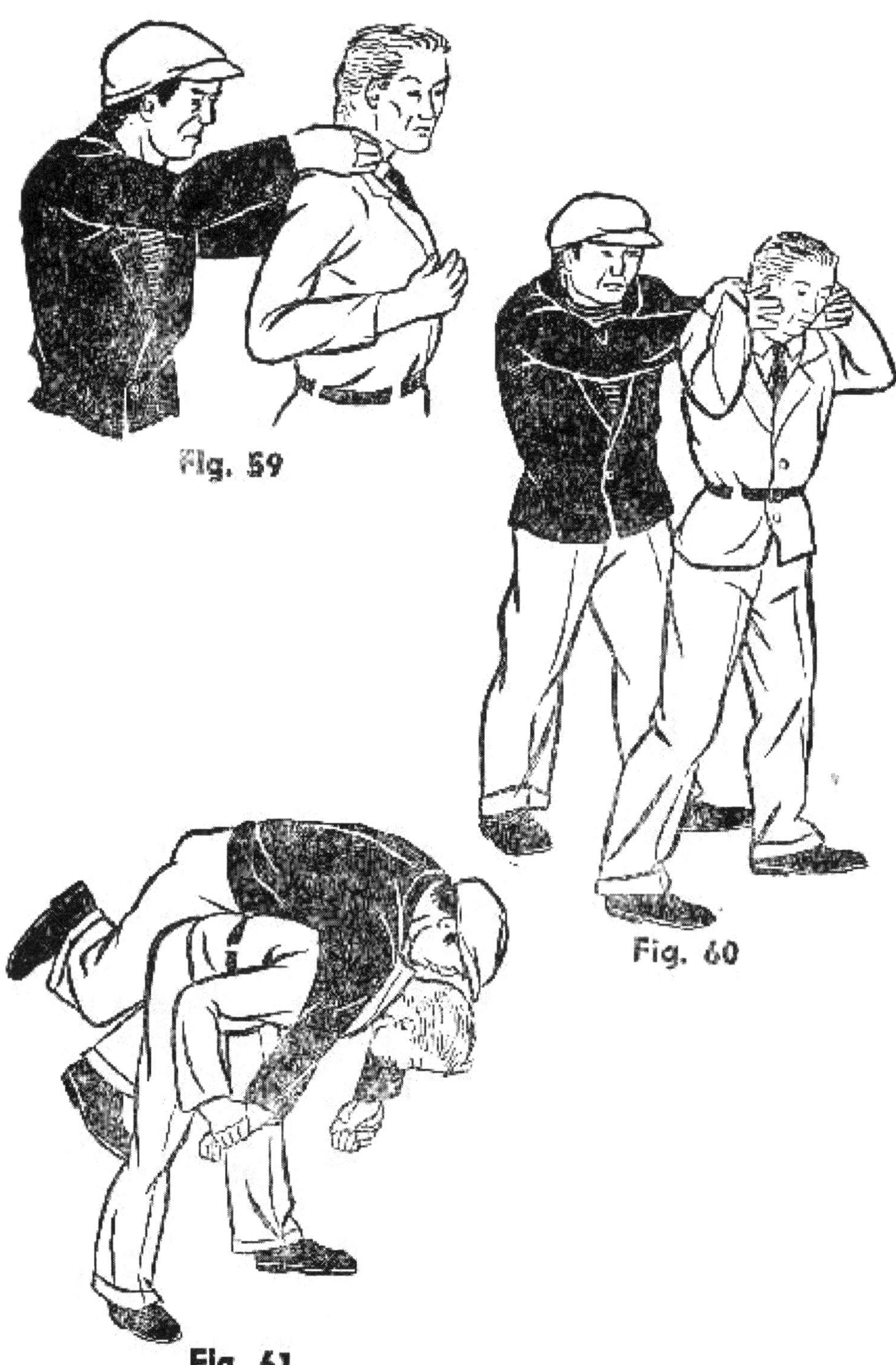

Fig. 59

Fig. 60

Fig. 61

## ANSWER TO A RIGHT HOOK

YOUR opponent is swinging a right fist at you.

1. Quickly move aside and, turning on your right foot, seize the upraised wrist in your right hand (Fig. 62).
2. Keep turning until you can slip your left arm over his shoulder, as in Fig. 63. Your weight is still on your right foot.
3. As he sways forward push him over, retaining your hold on his wrist (Fig. 64).

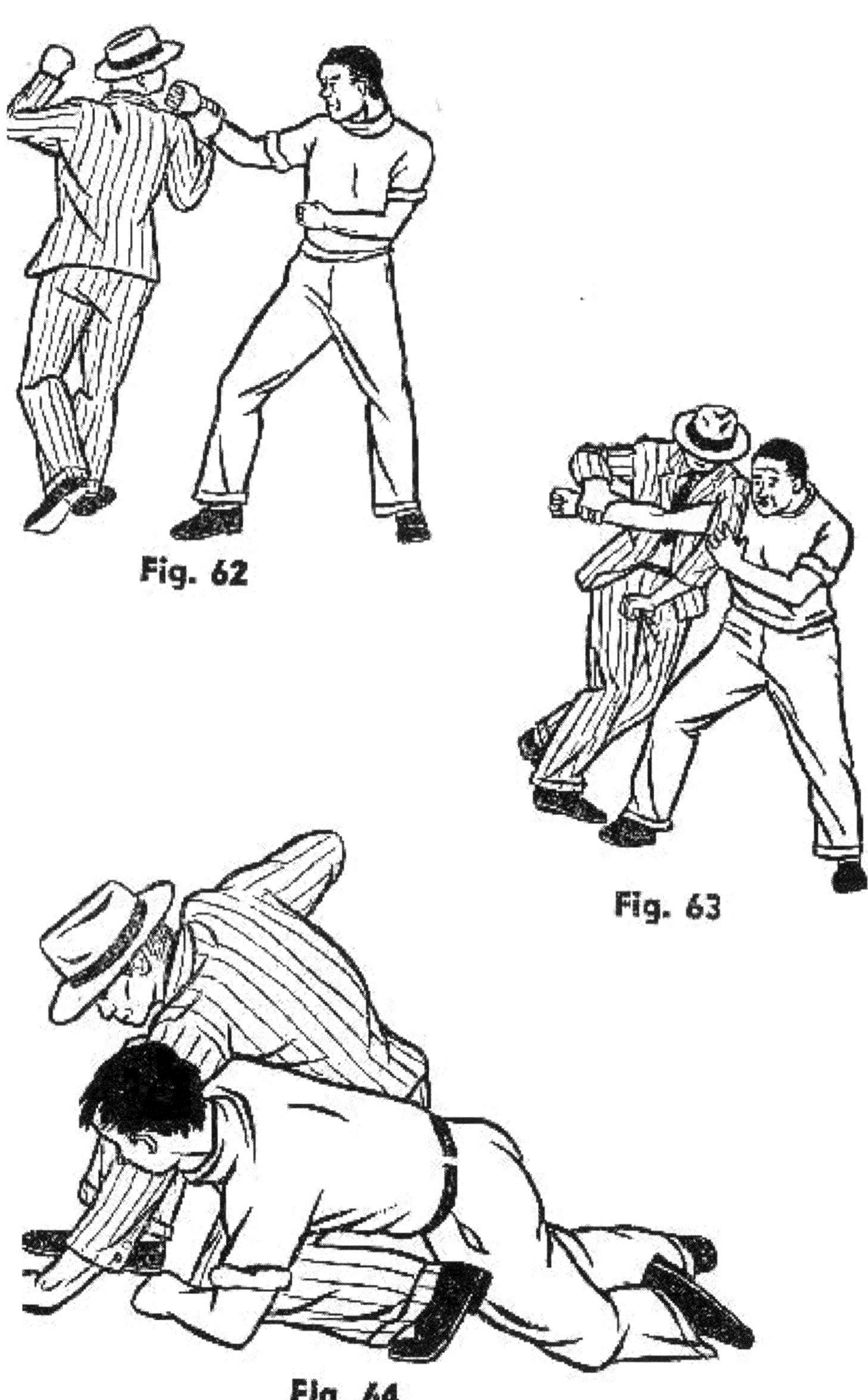

Fig. 62

Fig. 63

Fig. 64

## BREAKING A FULL-NELSON

YOU are caught in a full-nelson as in Fig. 65.

1. Seize your opponent's head, as in Fig. 66, and dip your knees.
2. Bend forward from the waist and, with a sudden jerk, spill him to the floor. His hold will be broken (Fig. 67).

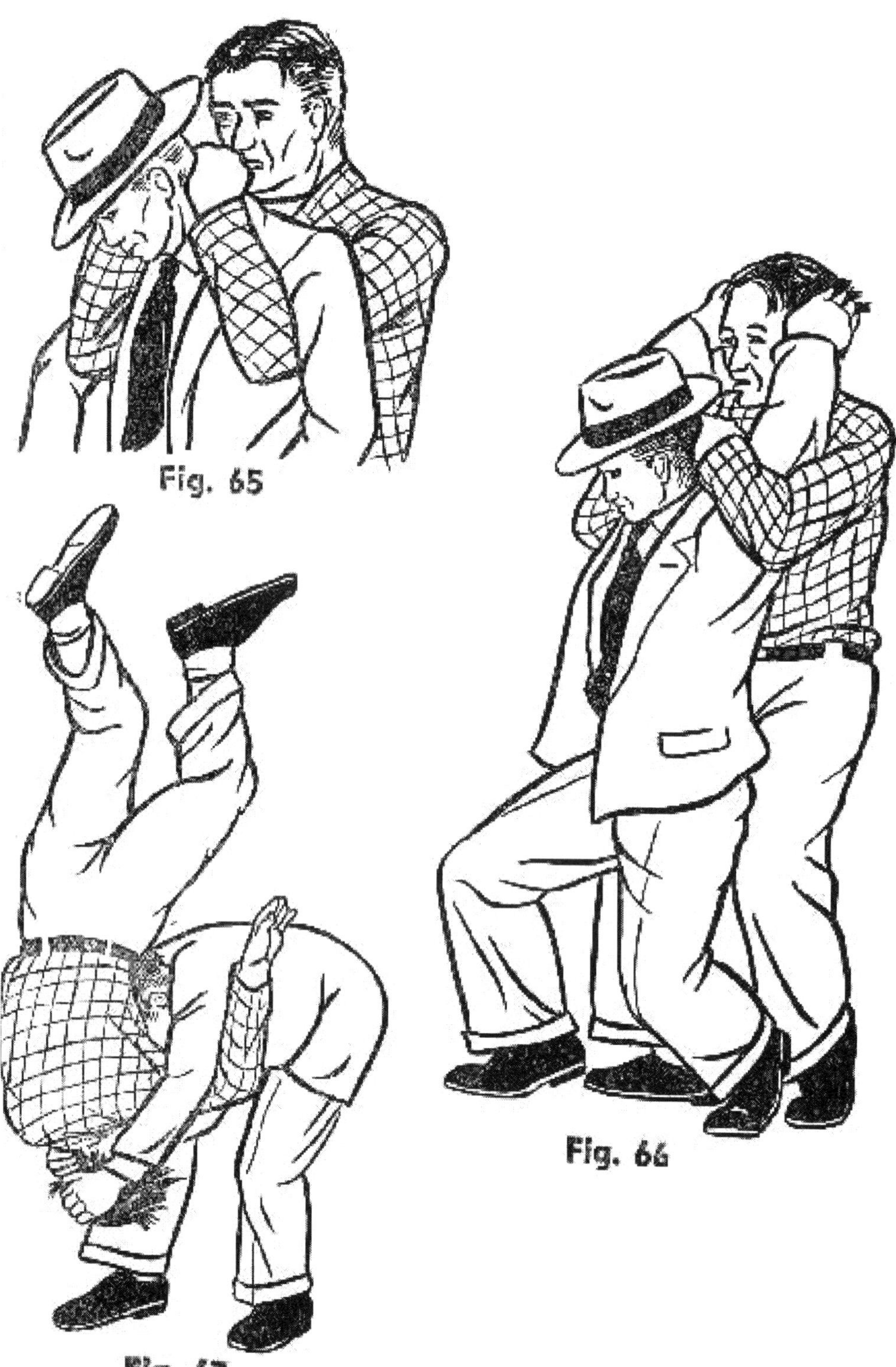

Fig. 65

Fig. 66

Fig. 67

# 6 *Thwarting An Armed Adversary*

## HOLDUP

A thug, flashing a gun, orders you to "stick 'em up."

1. Put up your hands instantly (Fig. 68). Throw him off-guard by acting frightened. Let him come close up. Watch for the moment when his attention slackens. Sometimes you can distract him momentarily with a couple of words, as "I won't resist—don't shoot."
2. With a sudden downward swoop of the right hand, catch his gun wrist from below, jerking it away from your body. Be sure to apply an underhand grip, i.e., thumb on top (Fig. 69).
3. Use your other hand to grasp the gun (Fig. 70).
4. Holding his wrist firmly push backward, wrenching the gun from his hand. You can break his grip with a sharp knee jab to his groin (Fig. 71).

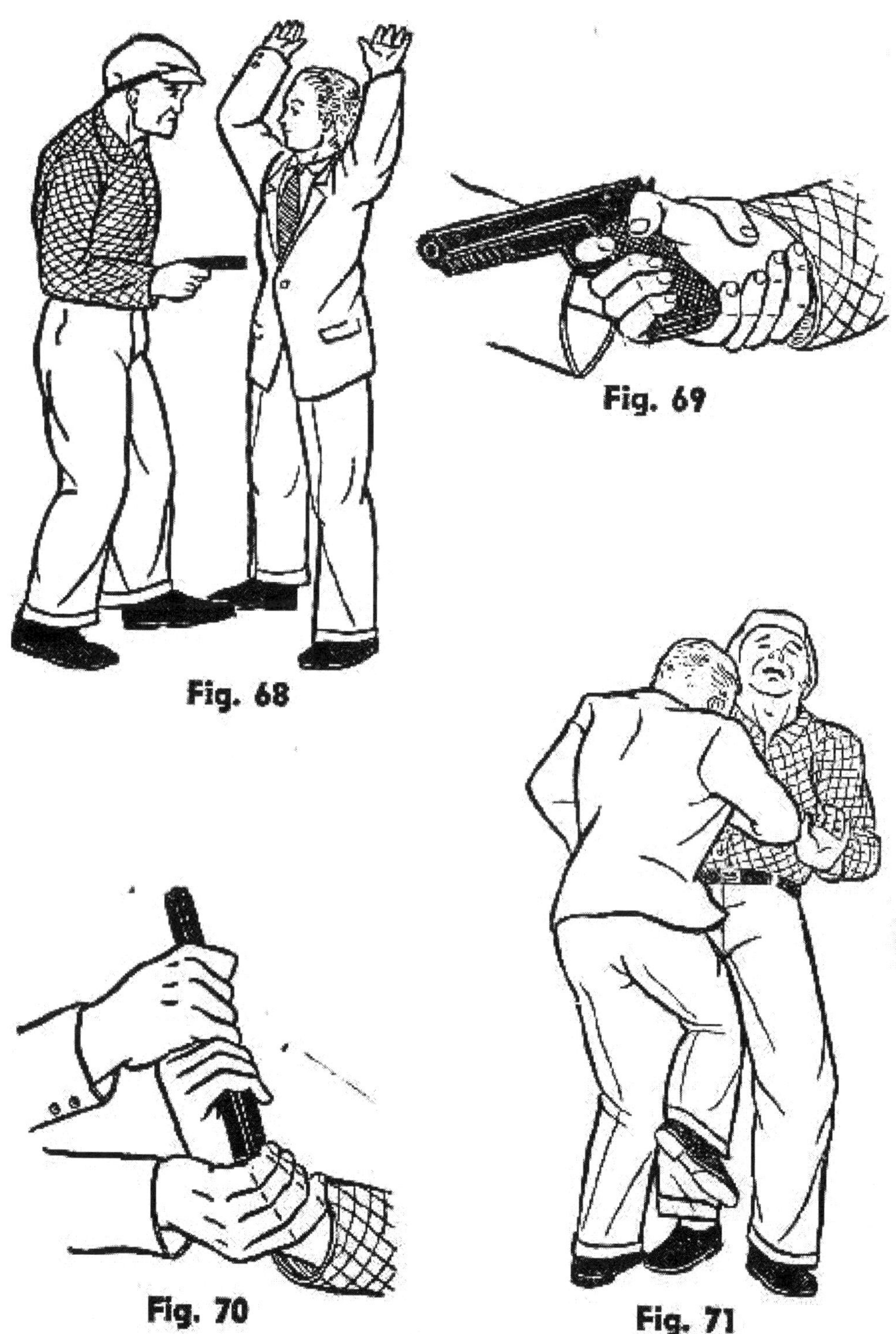

Fig. 68

Fig. 69

Fig. 70

Fig. 71

## HOLDUP (Gun at Your Back)

A gun is poked into your ribs.

1. Jerk your head right so as to glimpse your opponent over your shoulder (Fig. 72).
2. Whirling right suddenly, shove the gun aside with your elbow (Fig. 73).
3. Keep pivoting right, swinging your left fist to your opponent's jaw and warding off the gun with your other hand (Fig. 74).
4. As he falls, catch his gun wrist with your right hand (Fig. 75) and wrench the gun from him.

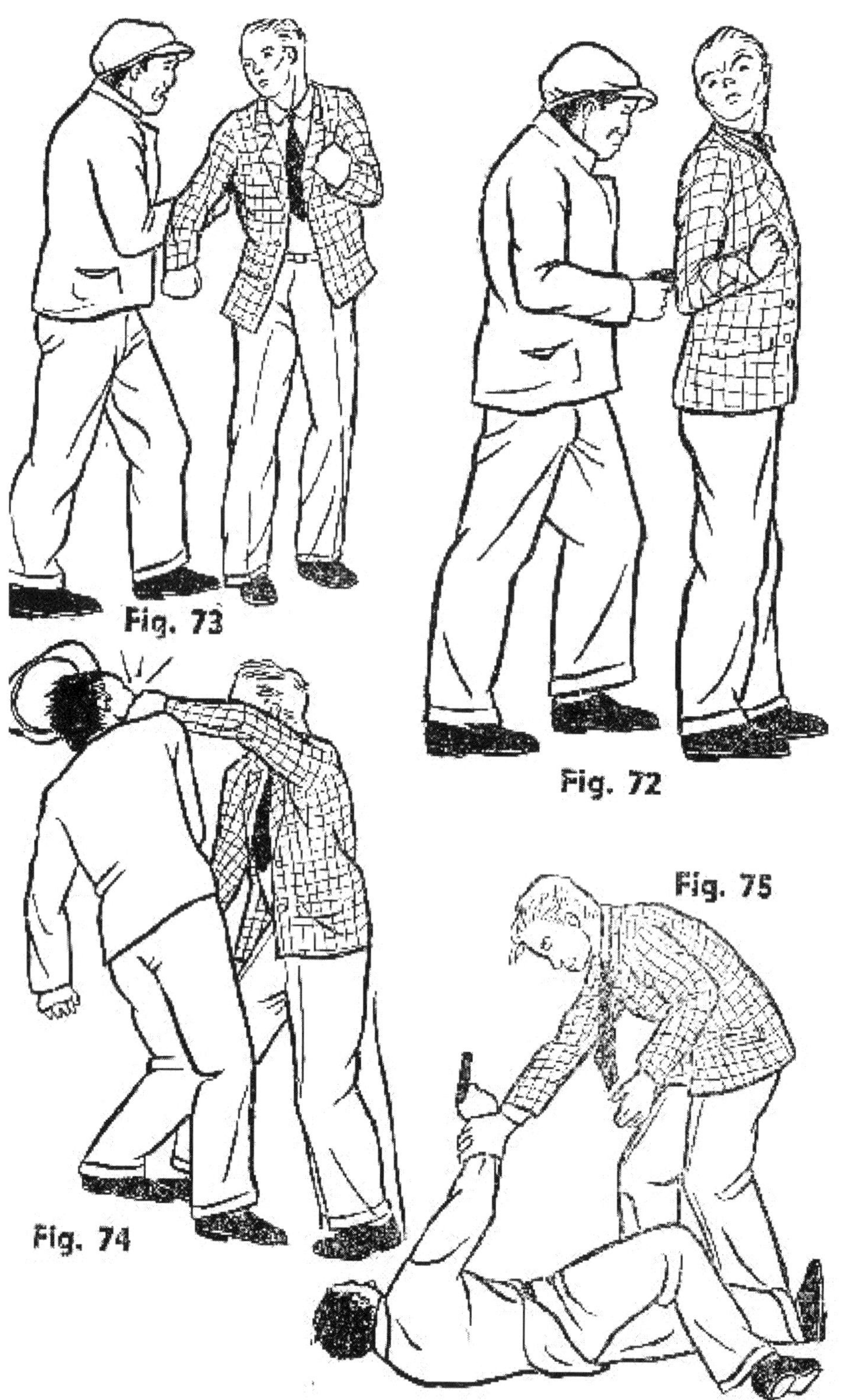

Fig. 73

Fig. 72

Fig. 74

Fig. 75

## KNIFE ATTACK

YOUR assailant lunges at you with a knife in his right hand.

1. Using your left hand, strike the descending wrist with a sharp edge-of-the-hand blow. At once close your hand around his wrist from below, so that your thumb is on the outside and points to the right (Fig. 76).
2. Keep forcing his arm out. He will be off-balance and will start sinking to his knees (Fig. 77).
3. Retain your grip when he falls. Then turn his hand at the elbow and force it inwards. He will have to release the knife (Fig. 78).

If you use a knife to practice this defense, be sure to cover the blade securely to avoid the possibility of accident.

Fig. 76

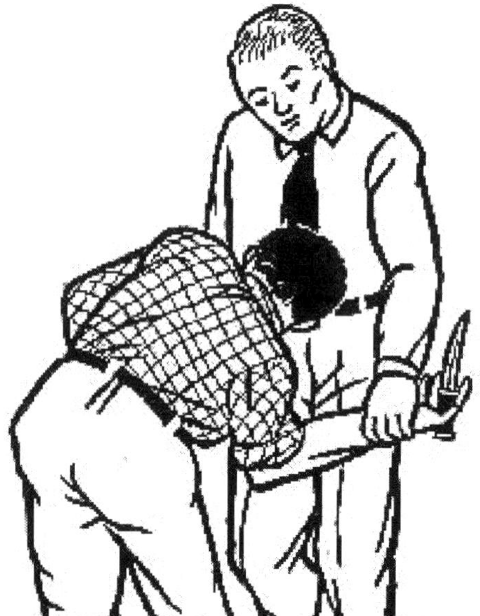

Fig. 77

Fig. 78

## CLUB ASSAULT

YOUR attacker is brandishing a club in his right hand.

1. Using your left hand, block the assault with an edge-of-the-hand blow to his wrist and immediately catch the wrist, keeping to the right. Jerk his wrist away from the body (Fig. 80).
2. Place your left foot in front of his right. Pull his arm forward and outward. He is now lurching because of the momentum of his original thrust. You can speed the process by shoving against his right shoulder with your free arm (Fig. 81).
3. The instant he falls, pin him down by pressing your left knee into his arm. Continue forcing his wrist until he drops the club (Fig. 82).

The same technique can be used to ward off an attack with a hammer or similar weapon.

Fig. 81

Fig. 80

Fig. 82

# 7 *Police and G-Men Favorites*

## POLICE "COME-ALONG"

"COME-ALONG" is a police term for the technique of marching a stubborn customer to the station house. You will find this method equally effective in getting a nuisance or a drunk out of your home, store, or office. A soldier, too, may escort his prisoner in this manner.

1. Using your right hand, seize your opponent's right wrist, give it a sudden wrench, and pull his arm away from his body (Fig. 83).
2. Wrap your upper left arm over his, just above the elbow, as in Fig. 84.
3. Bring your forearm under his elbow and secure the grip by grasping your own left wrist with your right hand (Fig. 85). You've got him now where you want him. Further resistance on his part would fracture his arm.

Fig. 83

Fig. 84

Fig. 85

## CHAIR TRICK

A person who suspects your intention to evict or bounce him may entrench himself in a chair, gripping the arms and holding on for dear life. Here's one way of getting him up in a hurry.

1. Seize his wrist with your left hand. Slip your right hand under his armpit and grasp a fold of clothing near the shoulder (Fig. 86).
2. As you apply upward pressure with your forearm, pull out your opponent's hand (Fig. 87).
3. This will make him get up. Then, by forcing his hand downward, as in Fig. 88, you will have him in a convenient "come-along."

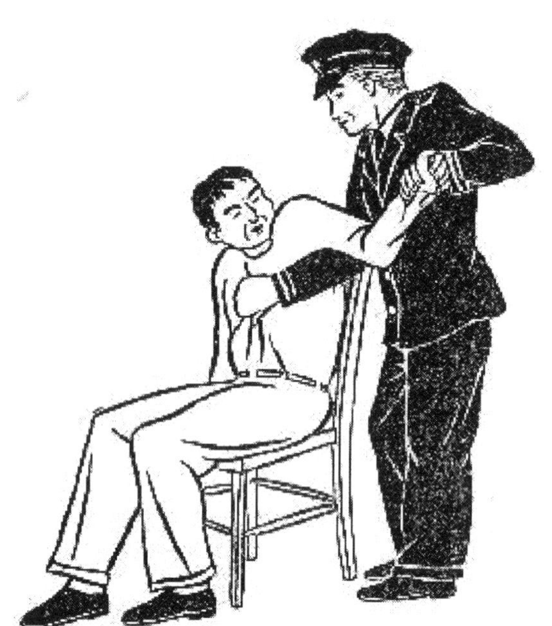

Fig. 86

Fig. 88

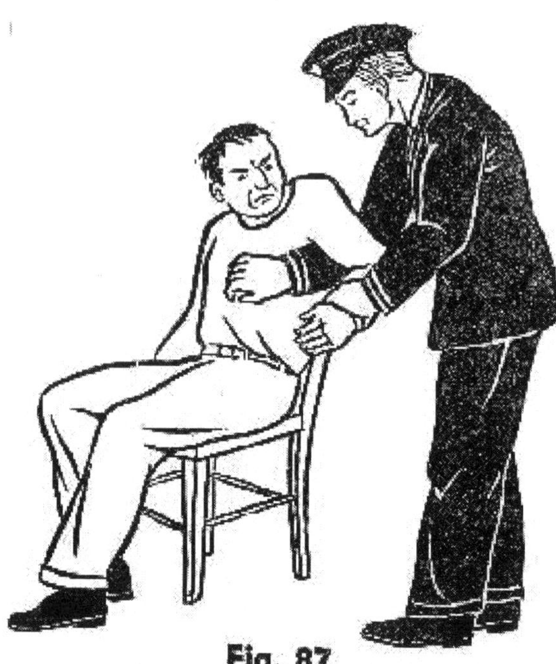

Fig. 87

## CORRALLING AN ESCAPING FOE

TO catch a fugitive who is running away from you:

1. Take off your jacket as you run, holding it in both hands.
2. As you get close to him, fling the jacket over his head (Fig. 89), and twist it around his neck. You can now handle him easily.

Fig. 89

# 8 Self-Defense For Women

## FREEDOM FROM FEAR

MANY a woman suffers untold anguish when forced to walk along dark, deserted streets or lonely roads. The night conjures up terrifying pictures. A dark figure suddenly detaching itself from the shadows. A man with brutish hands who may paw, attack, perhaps murder her. The mere thought sets her body trembling for she is only too well aware of her own helplessness.

Yet this fear can so easily be eliminated. A woman need not be an Amazon to defend herself. She can be equipped for any emergency with LIGHTNING JU-JITSU. All the techniques and defenses described in this book can be applied by a woman.

This section is specially included because women often have to face criminal assaults of a type that a man would not encounter. The remedies are simple—and well worth the learning.

## THE ANSWER TO PAWING HANDS

YOUR assailant is trying to paw you, as in Fig. 90.

1. Instead of drawing away as he expects you to, step on his foot—both, if they are together.

2. At the same moment shove his chin back forcefully with the heel of your hand (Fig. 91). He will fall back and may get a broken neck in the process.

Fig. 90

Fig. 91

## MOVIE MASHER MEDICINE

THE movie masher isn't exactly a menace, but he can spoil your whole evening unless you act firmly. Your problem is to get rid of him as quickly and quietly as possible.

One or more of the following methods is recommended:

1. If the seating arrangement permits it, jab your elbow sharply into his side (Fig. 92).
2. Using the hand farthest from him, deliver a two-finger jab to his abdomen (Fig. 93).
3. Gently lift his hand—he'll think you're responding to his advances—and, using both your hands, apply the thumbscrew (Fig. 94).

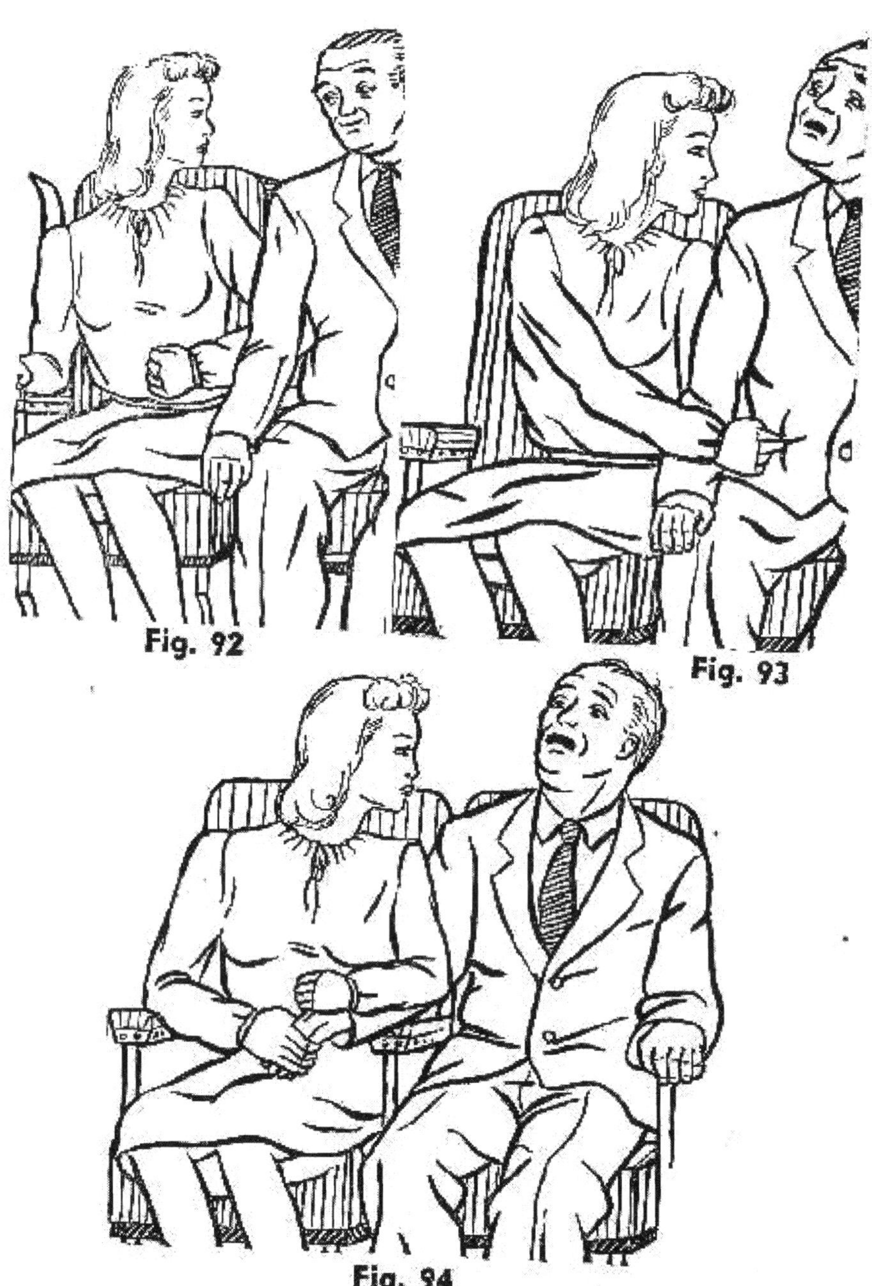

Fig. 92

Fig. 93

Fig. 94

## BREAKING A HAIR CLUTCH

YOUR assailant is dragging you backwards by the hair, as in Fig. 95.

1. Instead of resisting, let yourself be pulled up close to him.
2. Stooping suddenly, twist partly around and deliver an elbow jab to his kidney (Fig. 96).

The same defense may be used if anyone attempts to strangle you from behind.

Be very careful in practising, as the kidney blow may have fatal results.

Fig. 95

Fig. 96

## BREAKING AN UNWELCOME EMBRACE

YOUR assailant is crushing you against his body (Fig. 97).

1. Catch his chin with the heel of your right hand and shove back firmly. With your left fist, punch him in the small of the back. This action will throw him off-balance (Fig. 98).

2. Simultaneously, wedge your left foot in back of his right foot making sure that your heel touches his. He will fall backwards (Fig. 99).

If your hands are also caught in the grip, jab your knee into his groin until he is forced to relax his hold. Then proceed as above.

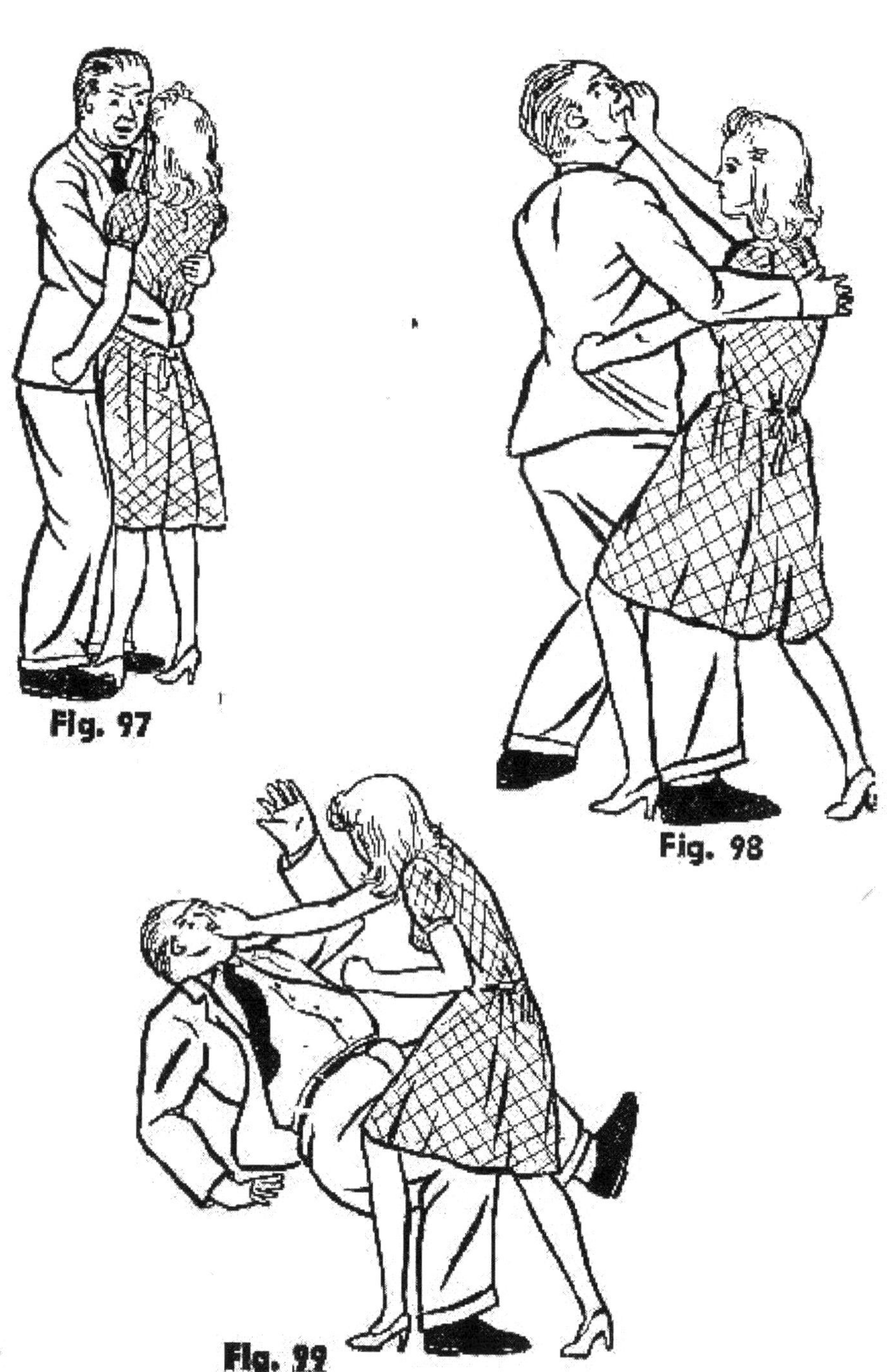

Fig. 97

Fig. 98

Fig. 99

# 9 Commando "Blitz" Tactics

## HOW TO DISARM AN ENEMY OF HIS TOMMY GUN

A tommy gun is pressed against your back.

1. Pivot right, shoving your right elbow back and up to deflect the muzzle of the gun upwards (Fig. 100).
2. Seize the muzzle with your right hand and the butt with your left, taking care to keep the muzzle pointed up (Fig. 101).
3. Trip your opponent by bringing your left foot behind his left knee. Since he is pulling backwards to retain possession of the gun, he will fall (Fig. 102).
4. Immediately yank the gun up and out of his hand (Fig. 103). His grip will be relaxed because of the unexpected loss of balance. With the gun in your possession, you are master of the situation. If necessary, bludgeon him into unconsciousness with the butt end.

The same defense may be used against an enemy with a sub-machine gun.

Fig. 100

Fig. 101

Fig. 102

Fig. 103

## STALKING A SENTRY

STALKING a sentry is a job requiring skill and nerve, for you are working behind enemy lines and the slightest mistake would probably prove fatal—for you. To stalk, remember, is to hunt with the intention of killing.

Should you get this assignment, here are some pointers:

Work in the dark, or semi-darkness. Camouflage your face and hands to avoid any reflection of light. Wear soft, noiseless shoes.

If you have confederates, arrange beforehand for some distraction at the time you plan to take the sentry. Any unusual noise—the tossing of a stone or a grenade, a drunken quarrel—would do the trick. Sometimes, with ingenuity and the proper materials, you might yourself rig up some mechanical distraction to go off at the right time.

Do not be in too much of a hurry. Watch your sentry closely before you approach. Be familiar with his clothing and equipment. Note where he is most vulnerable. Look for any physical peculiarities, such as uneven gait, etc. You may have to grapple with him later. See which way he turns when stopped. Steal up slowly from behind, advancing one foot at a time. A crouching position is best. Should he turn in your direction, do not move. He may not have seen you. Running away would only draw gunfire.

As soon as you are directly behind him, proceed to attack in one of the following ways:

1. **With a hammer or bludgeoning implement.** Strike a heavy blow on the head, the back of the neck, or between the shoulder blades (Fig. 104).
2. **With a knife or bladed instrument.** Cover his mouth with your left hand to stop an outcry while you plunge the blade into a vital spot (Fig. 105).
3. **With your hands.** Strangle him from behind (Fig. 106).

Fig. 104

Fig. 105

Fig. 106

## SENTRY DEFENSE AGAINST MUGGING

IF you are a sentry your enemy may try to sneak up to you from behind and mug you. Mugging is simply strangling from behind with the elbow. In such a case:

1. Twist your head sideways to lessen the pain (Fig. 107).
2. Flex your knees and grasp your opponent's jacket or shirt at the shoulder and elbow to give you leverage (Fig. 108).
3. Quickly bend forward from the waist, pulling him over your shoulder (Fig. 109).

Fig. 107

Fig. 108

Fig. 109

## SILENT WEAPONS

SHOULD you be working behind enemy lines as a scout, guerrilla, or for some other reason, you might have occasion to "dispatch" an enemy. Obviously, you would not carry rifle and bayonet on such a mission. You might not even be able to fire a pistol or depend on your fighting skill, since a shot or an outcry would betray your presence. What would you do?

The solution to this problem is found in recent and current experiences of guerrilla fighters in Spain, China, Yugoslavia and Russia. They tell of using "invisible" (easily concealed) weapons which can kill effectively—and in silence.

The following list is suggestive:

- Butt end of a pistol
- Club
- Hammer or small axe
- Length of pipe
- Handfull of coins sewn into a canvas bag
- Sock or stocking stuffed with sand
- Long ladies' hatpin
- Brass knuckles
- Knife, stiletto, dagger, or any other bladed instrument.
- Wire, cord, or even fishline (for strangling or tying)
- Handkerchief or cloth (for gag)

This list can easily be augmented, according to the materials at hand and the ingenuity of the soldier.

## Closing Thoughts

This material you studied should lead you to at least the following questions:

1. Why was the method and system created?
2. What were the social restrictions of the time and place?
3. What were the terrain limitations?
4. What clothing helped developed this art and what made this art ineffective?
5. What were the weapons used or not used and if so why?
6. The question should be would this martial art work well today or would need to be modified to today's time, social rules, terrains, and weapons?
7. What methods or techniques did you learn that could be used in your personal system or style?
8. How did the teacher/master apply their understanding of physics?
9. How did the teacher/master apply their understanding of anatomy?
10. How did the teacher/master apply their understanding of biology?

Understand by asking questions and seeking answers. You should be able incorporate the 21 concepts into your fighting system/ personal fighting style. Train to be in condition as well. This combination will make you will be a successful fighter. Train as if your life depends upon it. I hope that it never has to, stay safe out there and until next time.

Marc Lawrence

Master Teacher and Scientist

Made in the USA
Columbia, SC
19 July 2019